Into His Presence

Into His Presence

DAILY

DEVOTIONS

FOR

PRAYER

CROSSWAY BOOKS • WHEATON, ILLINOIS
A DIVISION OF GOOD NEWS PUBLISHERS

Into His Presence

Originally published by Fleming H. Revell
as *Practical Portions for the Prayer Life.*

Also previously published as *Daily Meditations for
Prayer,* copyright © 1978 by Good News Publishers.

First printing, *Into His Presence,* 1997

Published by Crossway Books
a division of Good News Publishers
1300 Crescent Street
Wheaton, Illinois 60187

Cover photo: The Image Bank

Cover design / Art direction: Cindy Kiple

Printed in the United States of America

ISBN 0-89107-967-X

Scripture quotations are generally taken from the *King
James Version,* though some (cited and uncited) are from
other translations.

Library of Congress Cataloging-in-Publication Data
Daily meditations for prayer.
   Into his presence : daily devotions for prayer
      p.   cm.
   Originally published: Daily meditations for prayer. Wheaton, Ill.:
Good News Publishers, © 1978.
   Includes index.
   ISBN 0-89107-967-X
   1. Devotional calendars. 2. Prayer—Christianity.   I. Title.
BV4810.D255   1997
242'.2—dc21   97-17759

05	04	03	02	01	00	99	98	97
15	14	13	12	11	10	9 8	7 6	5 4	3 2	1

Prelude

※

A man's words are like goads,
and his collected sayings are like nails driven home;
they put the mind of one man into many a life.

E C C L E S I A S T E S   1 2 : 1 1

M O F F A T

※

Throughout the history of the church, the spiritual lives of the Lord's people have been enriched by the special abilities of those who have spoken and written with comprehension and appreciation of the riches of God in Christ Jesus. Some of these were the authors of the meditations that make up this book. Some of their names have been household words for generations.

There can be no doubt that these men and women were gifted beyond the measure of most, since "one star differeth from another star in glory." Yet the heart is quick to sense that what motivated them all was intimacy of communion with Him "whom having not seen, they loved." Their spoken and written words reveal a personal experiencing of God, a reverence and godly fear, a holy wonder, which are rare indeed in this age.

Yet despite their spiritual depth and often majestic phraseology, these daily devotionals are practical portions for the Christian's prayer-life. For any who truly hunger and thirst after righteousness, whose souls thirst for God, for the living God, who have found with the Psalmist that "while I was musing the fire burned," this volume will be a standing invitation to a closer walk with God and a satisfying deepening of the miraculous experience of prayer.

PHILIP R. NEWELL

But we will give ourselves
continually to prayer.

A C T S   6 : 4

*I*t was an apostolic decision made at a time when the growth of the work demanded more workers and new plans. Others were appointed to attend to the new needs; the apostles gave themselves up more definitely and fully to the ministry of prayer and preaching. There is a ministry of prayer as well as a ministry of preaching, and however much there may seem to be an oversupply for the ministry of preaching there never has been an oversupply of men and women who have given themselves to the ministry of prayer. Here is an open door for God's children, an open door to great usefulness in the church and in the world. The field that may be occupied by prayer workers is practically limitless. It is a far larger field than can be occupied by any preacher. Any child of God can enter it, while those longest in it can always reach out to a larger usefulness in occupying it.

To help to a richer prayer-life, and to a deeper sense of its many privileges and responsibilities is the purpose of this selection of thoughts on prayer.

Watch unto prayer.

1   P E T E R   4 : 7

Praying always, and watching
thereunto with all perseverance.

E P H E S I A N S   6 : 1 8

*C*ommunion with God was never more needful
than now. Feverish activity rules in all spheres
of life. Christian effort is multiplied and systematized
beyond all precedent; and all those things make fellowship with God hard to compass. We are so busy
thinking, discussing, defending, inquiring, or preaching and teaching and working, that we have no time,
and no leisure of heart for quiet contemplation, without which the exercise of the intellect upon Christ's
truth will not feed, and busy activity in Christ's cause
may starve the soul.

A L E X A N D E R   M A C L A R E N

We must resolutely take time to pray, to get alone with
God. Satan will hinder us by crowding other things
into our life, if possible. We need daily to watch unto
prayer. Not only have regular seasons of prayer, but fill
in the life with many extra seasons. How much we
would gain if we would frequently give a few moments
to thinking of God without making any request.

*I have set the Lord always
before me: because He is at my
right hand, I shall not be moved.*

P S A L M   1 6 : 8

*G*et out of the ruts of prayer. Some of us can only pray in one way, and consequently we get tired of praying. The ruts of prayer are the deepest ruts in the world. Pray sometimes standing up; then pray kneeling; then pray sitting down; then pray lying down on your couch at night. Pray in the morning when the sun first streams in at your window. Pray at noonday when you stand up at the lunch counter in some big city. Pray at night when you go to the place of recreation. Never go to any place where prayer is impossible. Pray as you take the sleeper on the train at night, and the train rolls out of the big station into the darkness and unknown. . . . Pray sometimes alone when nobody hears. Then get some dear friend to kneel down and lead you in prayer, and when your lips are dry and your heart is dull that other friend may lift you up to God.

W. H. P. FAUNCE

Praying for some new object will help keep prayer out of ruts.

And it came to pass that, as He was praying in a certain place, when He ceased, one of His disciples said to Him, Lord, teach us to pray.

L U K E 1 1 : 1

*L*ord, teach us to pray. Yes, to pray. This is what we need to be taught. Though in its beginnings prayer is so simple that the feeblest child can pray, yet it is at the same time the highest and holiest work to which man can rise. It is fellowship with the Unseen and Most Holy One. The powers of the eternal world have been placed at its disposal. It is the very essence of true religion, the channel of all blessings, the secret of power and life. Not only for ourselves, but for others, for the church, for the world, it is to prayer that God has given the right to take hold of Him and His strength. It is on prayer that the promises wait for their fulfillment, the kingdom for its coming, the glory of God for its full revelation.

A N D R E W M U R R A Y

Pray to be taught deeper lessons in the school of prayer. Earnestly and diligently seek to learn those lessons, that your prayer-life may be intelligent, trustful, powerful.

Ask and it shall be given you; seek and ye shall find; knock, and it shall be opened unto you. For every one that asketh receiveth, and he that seeketh findeth; and to him that knocketh it shall be opened.

M A T T H E W   7 : 7 ,   8

*I*ntense practicalness characterizes the Scriptural idea of prayer. The Scriptures make it a reality and not a reverie. They never bury it in the notion of a poetic or philosophic contemplation of God. They do not merge it in the mental fiction of prayer by action in any other or all other duties of life. They have not concealed the fact of prayer beneath the mystery of prayer. . . . Up on the level of inspired thought, prayer is PRAYER—a distinct, unique, elemental power in the spiritual universe as pervasive, and as constant as the great occult powers of Nature.

AUSTIN PHELPS

Is prayer in my life the practical, powerful, helpful exercise that God intended it to be? Are my prayers really accomplishing anything in connection with God's kingdom? If not should I not begin today to learn how to prevail with God in prayer?

And Jesus answered and said unto him,
What wilt thou that I should do unto thee?

M A R K   1 0 : 5 1

*T*here is now still many a suppliant to whom the Lord puts the same question, and who cannot, until it has been answered, get the aid he asks. Our prayers must not be a vague appeal to His mercy, an indefinite cry for blessing, but the distinct expression of definite need. Not that His loving heart does not understand our cry, or is not ready to hear. But He desires it for our own sakes. Such definite prayer teaches us to know our own needs better. . . . It leads us to judge whether our desires are according to God's Word, and whether we really believe that we shall receive the things we ask. It helps us to wait for the special answer, and to mark it when it comes.

A N D R E W   M U R R A Y

What wilt thou? Lovingly does the Lord Jesus ask us, that we may order our prayers aright, and be purposeful and definite in our requests. What wilt thou today? Be free to ask for some definite blessing because Jesus invites you to.

According to your faith be it unto you.

MATTHEW 9:29

*W*e want to be more businesslike and use common sense with God in pleading promises. If you were to go to one of the banks and see a man go in and out and lay a piece of paper on the table, and take it up again and nothing more; if he did that several times a day, I think there would soon be orders to keep the man out. Those men who come to the bank in earnest present their cheques, they wait till they receive their gold and then they go, but not without having transacted real business. They do not put the paper down, speak about the excellent signature, and discuss the correctness of the document, but they want their money for it, and they are not content without it. These are the people who are always welcome at the bank and not the triflers. Alas, a great many people play at praying, it is nothing better. They do not expect God to give them an answer, and thus they are mere triflers, who mock the Lord.

C. H. SPURGEON

Our Heavenly Father would have us do real business with Him in our praying.

Ye ask and receive not, because ye ask amiss,
that ye may spend it in your pleasures.

J A M E S   4 : 3

When I come to God in prayer, He always looks to what the aim is of my petition. If it be merely for my comfort or joy I seek His grace, I do not receive. But if I can say that it is that He may be glorified in my dispensing His blessings to others, I shall not ask in vain. Or if I ask for others, but want to wait until God has made me so rich that it is no sacrifice or act of faith to aid them, I shall not obtain. But if I can say that I have already undertaken for my needy friend, that in my poverty I have already begun the work of love, because I know I have a Friend who would help me, my prayer will be heard.

A N D R E W   M U R R A Y

We need to learn in our prayer-life that it is God's plan to bless men in order that they may be a blessing. Prayer is answered not to be consumed on self but to be passed on. "Freely ye have received, freely give." Matthew 10:8. Read also Genesis 12:2; Psalm 67:1, 2. It is what we give that blesses rather than what we get.

*And when He had sent the multitude away,
He went up into a mountain apart to pray, and
when the evening was come, He was there alone.*
M A T T H E W 1 4 : 2 3

*T*he highest kind of prayer is too sacred to share with anyone but God. It is profoundly instructive to study the life of the Lord Jesus to find how often He went apart to pray. He could not let His most beloved disciples share His prayers. And this not only because the relation in which they stood to the Father was different from that in which He stood, but because His prayers were too deep, too sacred for them to know. When we have learned to agonize in prayer we will not tell our neighbors that we have learned it. But although we say nothing of it, its influence will be felt. It will inevitably touch our public prayers with a tenderness, and a yearning, and a pleading power as they never had before.

G E O R G E H . C . M A C G R E G O R

Going apart to pray means separating one's self from one's work, duties, service, for a time, for the special purpose of being much in prayer.

But thou, when thou prayest, enter into thy closet,
and when thou hast shut thy door, pray
to thy Father in secret.

M A T T H E W   6 : 6

*P*rayer is the most secret intercourse of the soul with God, and requires retirement, at least of the heart; for this is the closet in the house of God, which house is ourselves. Thither we retire, even in public prayer, and in the midst of company.

P A S Q U I E R   Q U E S N E L

Solitude is a means of spiritual education. Seek it; ordain it; cherish it; value it not for its own sake, but for faith's sake, and Christ's sake; sanctify your life by the prayers it will then inspire.

B I S H O P   H U N T I N G D O N

If our prayer-life is to be maintained with all freshness and vigor, there must be some place into which we can retire and be shut in alone with God, a place where we shall not be disturbed by the fear of others intruding, where we can indeed talk secretly and freely with the Lord. In this Christ is our example, for He was much alone with God in prayer.

*But thou, when thou prayest, enter into thine
inner chamber and having shut thy door,
pray to the Father which is in secret.*

M A T T H E W 6 : 6

*T*he first thing in closet prayer is: I must meet
my Father. The light that shines in the closet
must be: the light of the Father's countenance. The
fresh air from heaven with which Jesus would have it
filled, the atmosphere in which I am to breathe and pray,
is: God's Father-love, God's infinite Fatherliness. Thus
each thought or petition we breathe out will be simple,
hearty, childlike trust in the Father. This is how the
Master teaches us to pray: He brings us into the
Father's living presence. What we pray there must
avail. . . . To the man who withdraws himself from all
that is of the world and man, and prepares to wait
upon God alone, the Father will reveal Himself. As he
forsakes and gives up and shuts out the world, and the
life of the world, and surrenders himself to be led of
Christ into the secret of God's presence, the light of the
Father's love will light upon him.

A N D R E W M U R R A Y

Cause me to know the way wherein I should walk;
for I lift up my soul unto thee.

P S A L M   1 4 3 : 8

*I*n a time of change and crisis, we need to be much in prayer, not only on our knees, but in that sweet form of inward prayer, in which the spirit is constantly offering itself up to God, asking to be shown His will; soliciting that it may be impressed upon its surface, as the heavenly bodies photograph themselves on prepared paper. Wrapt in prayer like this, the trustful believer may tread the deck of the ocean steamer night after night, sure that He who points the stars to their courses will not fail to direct the soul which has no other aim than to do His will.

One good form of prayer at such a juncture is to ask that doors may be shut, that the way may be closed, and that all enterprises which are not according to God's will may be arrested at their beginning.

F. B. MEYER

We bring upon ourselves many a sorrow by preferring our own way to God's. His will is the way of peace and highest blessedness.

Casting all your care upon Him;
for He careth for you.

1   P E T E R   5 : 7

*W*hatsoever it is that presses thee, tell thy
Father; put over the matter into His hand,
and so thou shalt be freed from that dividing, perplexing care that the world is full of. When thou art either
to do or suffer anything, when thou art about any purpose or business, tell God of it, and acquaint Him with
it; yea, burden Him with it, and thou hast done for matter of caring; no more care, but quiet, sweet diligence
in thy duty, and dependence on Him for the carriage
of thy matters. Roll thy cares, and thyself with them,
as one burden, all on God.

L E I G H T O N

One of the most blessed lessons in the school of
prayer is learning to commit things definitely to the
Lord, and trustfully leaving them there. Art thou doing
this with thy burden, or with thy special need? Psalm
37:5

This lesson can only be learned through much
practice. Begin today to learn it.

*And the Lord said unto Moses, Wherefore
criest thou unto Me? speak unto the children
of Israel, that they go forward.*

E X O D U S   1 4 : 1 5

❋

*S*ome things you can obtain by work without
prayer; some things you can obtain by
prayer without other work; some things by the combi-
nation of working and praying: but no things at all
without your cooperation; and cooperation by prayer
has no kind of rational difficulty attendant upon it
which does not attend equally upon cooperation by
the method of work.

C .   G O R E

God taught Moses at the Red Sea, as He has many
times taught His people since, that there are times
when action is more necessary than prayer. When a
wealthy Christian proposed to Mr. Moody that they
pray for a certain sum of money needed for the Lord's
work, Mr. Moody replied, "Hadn't you better just give
that yourself and not trouble the Lord about it?" Prayer
was never meant to encourage idleness. Neither should
intense activity lessen prayerfulness.

Brethren, my heart's desire and prayer
to God for Israel is, that they might be saved.
R O M A N S   1 0 : 1

*L*et a man define to his own mind an object of prayer, and then let him be moved by desires for that object which impel him to pray, because he cannot otherwise satisfy the irrepressible longings of his soul; let him have such desires as shall lead him to search out, and dwell upon, and treasure in his heart, and return to again, and appropriate to himself anew, the encouragements to prayer, till his Bible opens of itself to the right places—and think you that such a man will have occasion to go to his closet, or come from it, with the sickly cry, Why, oh! why is my intercourse with God so irksome to me.

A U S T I N   P H E L P S

Do you really desire the things for which you pray; is your heart set upon them so that you say, "I will not let Thee go except Thou bless me"?

When we delight in the Lord (Psalm 37:4) Jesus will say to us as Jonathan said to David: "Whatsoever thy soul desireth I will even do it for thee." 1 Samuel 20:4

Remember me, O Lord,
with the favour that Thou bearest
unto Thy people:
O visit me with Thy salvation.

P S A L M 1 0 6 : 4

A prayer for self is not by any means necessarily a selfish prayer. We may pray for
something for ourselves in order that God may be glorified by our receiving it. (John 17:1; Psalm 50:15.) If we
would pray more for ourselves God would be more
glorified in us, and we would be a greater blessing to
others. It was well for the world that Jesus spent so
much time in prayer for Himself. If we would be fit to
pray for others we must spend much time in prayer for
ourselves. It is a bad sign when one is always praying
for others and never for himself. He is not like his
Master.

R. A. TORREY

We cannot be a blessing beyond the measure that we
receive a blessing. While praying for ourselves we
should have an eye on the needs of others, so that in
praying for ourselves we shall be securing others' good.

True prayer begins with looking in to see one's own
condition, but it issues in looking out to see the condition of others.

*I will direct my prayer
unto Thee, and will look up.*

P S A L M   5 : 3

*I*f we merely read our English version, and want an explanation of these two sentences, we find it in the figure of an archer, "I will direct my prayer unto Thee." I will put my prayer upon the bow, I will direct it toward heaven, and then when I have shot up my arrow I will look up to see where it has gone. But the Hebrew has a still fuller meaning than this—"I will direct my prayer." It is the word that is used for the laying in order of the wood and the pieces of the victim upon the altar, and it is used also for putting of the shewbread upon the table. It means just this: "I will arrange my prayer before Thee." I will lay it out upon the altar in the morning, just as the priest lays out the morning sacrifice. "I will marshall up my prayers," I will put them in order, call up all my powers, and bid them stand in their proper places, that I may pray with all my might and pray acceptably. "And will look up" or as the Hebrew might better be translated, "I will look out," I will look out for the answer.

C .   H .   S P U R G E O N

*For through Him we both have access
by one Spirit unto the Father.*

E P H E S I A N S   2 : 1 8

*L*et it be our comfort and strength to be assured that in the eternal fellowship of the Father and the Son, the power of prayer has its origin and certainty, and that through our union with the Son, our prayer is taken up and can have its influence in the inner life of the Blessed Trinity. God's decrees are no iron framework against which man's liberty would vainly seek to struggle. No. God Himself is the Living Love, who in His Son as man has entered into the tenderest relation with all that is human, who through the Holy Spirit takes up all that is human into the divine life of love, and keeps Himself free to give every human prayer its place in the government of the world.

A N D R E W   M U R R A Y

Prayer has power because it brings the believing soul into oneness with the operation of God the Father, the Son, and the Holy Spirit. John 14:12–14; Romans 8:26. Prayer is therefore a partnership and cooperation with the Trinity. How very essential is our part in that partnership and cooperation.

And He said, Thy name shall be called no more Jacob, but Israel: for as a prince has thou power with God and with men, and hast prevailed.

G E N E S I S   3 2 : 2 8

More things are wrought by prayer
Than this world dreams of. Wherefore let thy voice
Rise like a fountain for me night and day
For what are men better than sheep or goats,
That nourish a blind life within the brain,
If, knowing God, they lift not hands of prayer,
Both for themselves and those who call them friend!
For so the whole round earth is every way
Bound by gold chains about the feet of God.

T E N N Y S O N

These "gold chains" need to be greatly multiplied, for there are many subtle forces at work to drag "the whole round earth" away from God. Help, brother, help to increase these precious chains that bind the world to God, not only by the development of a deeper prayer-life for thyself, but interest others in developing a greater prayer movement in the church. Form some new chain today binding some soul, some church, some missionary or mission field to the throne of God.

For as the body without the spirit is dead,
so faith without works is dead also.

J A M E S   2 : 2 6

*P*rayer must never be made an excuse for idleness and sloth. Its design is to rouse to effort, by the hope of a divine blessing. Not until we are shut up to a difficulty which we can in no way touch, may we rely upon prayer alone. In the matter of personal sanctification, the exhortation is to watch and pray. A significant implication is found in Christ's words: "I have chosen you and ordained you that ye should go and bring forth fruit; and that your fruit should remain; that whatsoever ye shall ask the Father in My name He may give it you." John 15:16. Thus Jesus made labor a condition of acceptable prayer, as being a manifestation of sincerity, earnestness and self-denial, and as tending to the highest good of ourselves and others. He Himself labored and prayed, and taught His disciples so to do.

W I L L I A M   W.   P A T T O N

The story of Nehemiah beautifully illustrates this.

*And I will pour upon the house of David,
and upon the inhabitants of Jerusalem, the spirit
of grace, and of supplications.*

Z E C H A R I A H 1 2 : 1 0

*E*very new Pentecost has had its preparatory period of supplication—of waiting for enduement; and sometimes the time of tarrying has been lengthened from "ten days" to as many weeks, months, or even years; but never has there been an outpouring of the Divine Spirit from God without a previous outpouring of the human spirit toward God. To vindicate this statement would require us to trace the whole history of missions, for the field of such display of divine power covers the ages. Yet every missionary biography, from those of Eliot and Edwards, Brainerd and Carey, down to Livingstone and Burns, Hudson Taylor and John E. Clough, tells the same story: prayer has been the preparation for every new triumph; and so, if greater triumphs and successes lie before us, more fervent and faithful praying must be their forerunner and herald!

A . T . P I E R S O N

*Be merciful unto me, O God, be merciful
unto me: for my soul trusteth in Thee; yea, in the
shadow of Thy wings will I make my refuge,
until these calamities be overpast.*

P S A L M   5 7 : 1

When prayer has preceded trial, the trial turns out to be much less than we anticipated. The women found, when they reached the sepulchre, that the dreaded stone had been rolled away. When Peter reached the outer gate, that threatened to be an insurmountable obstacle to liberty, it opened to him of its own accord. So Jacob dreaded that meeting with Esau; but when Esau came up with him, he ran to meet him, and embraced him, and fell on his neck, and kissed him; and they wept. The heroic Gordon used to say that, in his lonely camel rides, he often in prayer encountered and disarmed chiefs, before he rode, unaccompanied, into their presence. None can guess, if they have not tried it for themselves, what a solvent prayer is for the difficulties and agonies of life.

F. B. M E Y E R

Pray one for another.

J A M E S   5 : 1 6

*T*he sincere worshipper is not to consider himself as a single or separate being, confining his concern wholly to himself. Our Saviour has initiated us into a more noble and enlarged spirit of devotion, when He taught us to begin with praying that the kingdom of God may be advanced over all, and that mankind may be rendered as happy by doing His will as the angels are in heaven. When we bow our knee to the common Father, let it be like affectionate members of His family, desiring the prosperity of all the brethren. . . . Our enemies themselves ought not to be forgotten in our prayers: . . . our prayers ought to be an exercise of extensive benevolence of heart; a solemn testimony offered up to the God of love, of our kind and charitable affection for all men.

H U G H   B L A I R

The territory embraced by our prayers should extend from nearest neighbors to the uttermost heathen. Pray for ALL men. 1 Timothy 2:1

It is well also to let others know sometimes that we are praying for them. This will encourage their faith and stimulate them to pray.

*I sought for a man that should stand
in the gap before Me for the land, that I should
not destroy it: but I found none.*

E Z E K I E L   2 2 : 3 0

*G*od seeks intercessors. He longs to dispense larger blessings. He longs to reveal His power and glory as God, His saving love more abundantly. He seeks intercessors in larger number, in greater power, to prepare the way of the Lord. He seeks them. Where could He seek them but in His Church? And how does He expect to find them? He entrusted to His Church the task of telling of their Lord's need, the task of encouraging and training, and preparing them for His holy service. And He ever comes again, seeking fruit, seeking intercessors.

Beloved fellow-Christians! God needs, greatly needs, priests who can draw near to Him, who live in His presence, and by their intercessions draw down blessings on others.

A N D R E W   M U R R A Y

And for this blessed work shall not you and I reply—
"Here am I, Lord, I yield myself to Thee and to the
Holy Spirit to serve in the ministry of intercession."

*Always in every prayer of mine for you
all making request with joy, for your fellowship
in the gospel from the first day until now.*

P H I L I P P I A N S   1 : 4 ,   5

*T*here are Christian people whose life is so far removed from excitement, agitation and peril, that they seem to have no opportunities for winning great moral victories; their powers are very limited, and they are not appointed to tasks of great difficulty and honor. Let them resolve to have their part in the righteousness of their comrades who face the fiercest dangers, and in the fame of the very chiefs and heroes of the great army of God. Let them pray for "all the saints," and their prayers will give courage, endurance, and invincible fidelity to those who are struggling with incessant temptations. . . . By constant and earnest intercession for "all the saints," those who are living in quiet and obscure places may share the honors and victories of all their comrades, may have some part in the praise of their holiness, and some part in their final reward.

R. W. DALE

Have you a list of God's servants for whom you daily pray?

The Lord my God will enlighten my darkness.

PSALM 18 : 28

*Quicken us, and we will
call upon Thy name.*

PSALM 80 : 18

*The letter killeth,
but the Spirit giveth life.*

2 CORINTHIANS 3 : 6

*P*rayer vitalizes the best truths. It refines the ore of Christian doctrine and leaves behind the true gold. Truth that can be prayed is truth that is newly tested and minted. The creed that ministers to true prayer is thereby the proven creed. We see further into spiritual truth on our knees than when standing highest on our feet. Heart then leads head as it was made to do. If God has an arrangement for hearing and answering prayer it must tend to vitalize all His best truths for us. In this way He can get Himself believed with a profound and living faith.

D. W. FAUNCE

Prayer and the Word of God are intimately related. We cannot have the one without the other. If we would pray we must study the Word; if we would understand the Word we must pray.

Have mercy upon me, O God, according to Thy lovingkindness: according unto the multitude of Thy tender mercies blot out my transgressions.

P S A L M 5 1 : 1

*F*aith's pleas are plentiful, and this is well, for faith is placed in divers positions and needs them all. She hath many needs, and having a keen eye she perceives that there are pleas to be urged in every case. I will not, therefore, tell you all faith's pleas, but I will just mention some of them, enough to let you see how abundant they are. Faith will plead all the attributes of God. "Thou art just, therefore spare Thou the soul for whom the Saviour died. Thou art merciful, blot out my transgressions. Thou art good, reveal Thy bounty to Thy servant. Thou art immutable, Thou has done thus and thus to others of Thy servants, do thus to me. Thou art faithful, canst Thou break Thy promise, canst Thou turn away from Thy covenant?" Rightly viewed all the perfections of Deity become pleas for faith.

C. H. SPURGEON

Prayer finds its greatest inspiration in God Himself.

*Because Thy lovingkindness is better than
life, my lips shall praise Thee.*

PSALM 63:3

Since God's lovingkindness is better than life,
the soul that possesses Him can have no
unappeased cravings, nor any yet hungry affections or
wishes. In the region of communion with God fruition
is contemporaneous with and proportioned to desire.
When the rain comes in the desert, what was baked
earth is soon rich pasture, and the dry torrent beds,
where the white stones glittered ghastly in the sunshine, are musical with rushing streams and fringed
with budding oleanders. On that telegraph a message
is flashed upward and an answer speeds downward, in
a moment of time. Many of God's gifts are delayed by
Love; but the soul that truly desires Him has never long
to wait for a gift that equals its desire.

ALEXANDER MACLAREN

Thou art coming to a King
Large petitions with thee bring,
For His grace and power are such
None can ever ask too much.

*Let us come before His presence with thanksgiving,
and make a joyful noise unto Him with psalms.*

P S A L M   9 5 : 2

*C*an we expect future mercies, if we are not thankful for past blessings? If a spirit of discontent and murmur is in our hearts, as though God had not dealt kindly with us, are we in a frame to approach Him, and implore His continued protection? Or if we accept His gifts so lightly, and as a matter of course, that we are not impressed with His goodness, have we not missed their principal benefit, and thus disqualified ourselves to ask or receive added favors? It is not by accident that the Psalms of David are half petition and half thanksgiving.

W I L L I A M   W .   P A T T O N

It is an exceedingly profitable devotional exercise, and very helpful to the prayer-life, to sometimes give the entire season one spends before God to praise and thanksgiving, not asking but just remembering and thanking God for His many blessings. For as ingratitude paralyzes the prayer-life, so thanksgiving nourishes it and opens the channels for richer blessings.

*He that believeth on Me, he shall do greater
works, because I go to the Father; and whatsoever ye
shall ask in My name, that will I do.*

J O H N   1 4 : 1 2 ,   1 3

*H*is going to the Father would give Him a
new power to hear prayer. For the doing
of the greater works, two things were needed: His
going to the Father to receive all power, our prayer in
His name to receive all power from Him again. As He
asks the Father, He receives and bestows on us the
power of the new dispensation for the greater works;
as we believe, and ask in His name, the power comes
and takes possession of us to do the greater works.

He that would do the works of Jesus must pray in
His name. He that would pray in His name must work
in His name.

A N D R E W   M U R R A Y

Christ's workers need not be without power; their
efforts need not be ineffectual. What we need is proper
adjustment by prayer to the source of all power, and
then the greater works will be done. "For it is God that
worketh in you."

For I know the thoughts that I think toward you, saith the Lord, thoughts of peace, and not of evil, to give you an expected end. Then shall ye call upon Me, and ye shall go and pray unto Me, and I will hearken unto you.

JEREMIAH 29:11, 12

*P*rayers of saints, offered in holy agreement, ascend like vapors, which blend and mingle in pure white clouds. The great Intercessor at the Throne presents them before God, made acceptable by His own infinite merit, and thus they prevail. The power of God is put at the disposal of praying souls; and upon the earth wonderful changes, convulsions, upheavings, revolutions take place. Prayer has gone up to heaven, found acceptance, and returned in answers of almighty power, as moisture goes up in vapor and returns in rain. Supplication, when it is according to scriptural conditions, commands divine interposition.

A. T. PIERSON

Study the story of the Apostolic Church, the story of missions since, the life of George Muller, and of many others of God's praying servants, and learn how marvelously prayer has shaped the history of the church, and wrought wonders among men.

*Thus saith the Lord God: I will yet for this be
inquired of by the house of Israel, to do it for them.*

E Z E K I E L   3 6 : 3 7

*P*rayer is part of the system of cooperation between God and man which pervades nature and life. No crop waves over the autumn field, no loaf stands on our breakfast table, no metal performs its useful service, no jewel sparkles on the brow of beauty, no coal burns in hearth or furnace, which does not witness to this dual workmanship of God and man. So in the spiritual world there must be cooperation, though on the part of man it is often limited to prayers, which may seem faint and feeble, but which touch the secret springs of Deity; as the last pick of the miner may break open a fountain of oil or a cavern set with dazzling jewels.

F . B . M E Y E R

Seeing so much depends on prayer let us never neglect this cooperation with God which God has ordained for us. Let us remember that if our part is left out the law will not operate and the blessing will not come.

*What things soever ye desire, when ye pray, believe that
ye receive them, and ye shall have them.*

M A R K   1 1 : 2 4

*H*ere we have a summary of the teaching of
our Lord Jesus on prayer. Nothing will so
much help to convince us of the sin of our remissness
in prayer, to discover its causes and to give us courage
to expect entire deliverance, as the careful study and
then the believing acceptance of that teaching. The
more heartily we enter into the mind of our blessed
Lord, and set ourselves simply just to think about
prayer as He thought, the more surely will His words
be as living seeds. They will grow and produce in us
their fruit—a life and practice exactly corresponding to
the divine truth they contain.

A N D R E W   M U R R A Y

Christ is our example, and in nothing is it more important that we should follow Him, than in His prayer-life.
For nothing do we need more constantly to sit at the
feet of Jesus and learn of Him than concerning prayer.
Oh to pray with something of His Spirit and earnestness, and fellowship with God and faith.

*Yea, in the way of Thy judgments, O Lord,
have we waited for Thee; the desire of our soul is to
Thy name, and to the remembrance of Thee. With my
soul have I desired Thee in the night.*

ISAIAH 26:8, 9

*D*esire is the secret power that moves the whole world of living men, and directs the course of each. And so desire is the soul of prayer, and the cause of insufficient or unsuccessful prayer is very much to be found in the lack or feebleness of desire. Some may doubt this: they are sure that they have very earnestly desired what they ask. But if they consider whether their desire has indeed been as whole-hearted as God would have it, they may come to see that it was indeed that lack of desire which was the cause of failure. "Ye shall seek Me and shall find when ye shall search for Me with all your heart."

ANDREW MURRAY

Desires will flow into the heart as the result of a careful consideration of our needs and the needs of others. Men desire what they feel they need. Think of the needs of men and desire great things for them.

Thy prayer of the upright is His delight.

P R O V E R B S   1 5 : 8

*S*ome people seem to regard prayer as the rehearsal of a set form of words, learned largely from the Bible or a liturgy; and when uttered they are only from the throat outward. Genuine prayer is a believing soul's direct converse with God. Phillips Brooks has condensed it into four words—a "true wish sent Godward." By it, adoration, thanksgiving, confession of sin, and petitions for mercies and gifts ascend to the throne, and by means of it infinite blessings are brought down from heaven. The pull of our prayer may not move the everlasting throne, but—like the pull on a line from the bow of a boat—it may draw us into closer fellowship with God, and fuller harmony with His wise and holy will.

T H E O D O R E   L .   C U Y L E R

More and more we must learn what the spirit of true prayer is. When we have learned that, the form of prayer will be cared for. The prayer-life will be best sustained when we are more and more concerned about the spirit than the form of prayer.

*They run and prepare themselves without
my fault: awake to help me, and behold. Thou
therefore, O Lord God of hosts, the God of Israel,
awake to visit all the heathen.*

P S A L M   5 9 : 4 ,   5

*T*he singer makes haste to grasp God's hand,
because he feels the pressure of the wind
blowing in his face. It is wise to break off the contemplation of enemies and dangers by crying to God.
Prayer is a good interruption of a catalogue of perils.
The petitions in verse 5 are remarkable, both in their
accumulation of the divine names and in their apparent transcending of the supplicant's need. The former
characteristic is no mere artificial or tautological heaping together of titles, but indicates repeated acts of
faith, and efforts of contemplation. Each name suggests something in God which encourages hope, and
when appealed to by a trusting soul, moves Him to act.

A L E X A N D E R   M A C L A R E N

Contemplation of God as revealed in His names cannot fail to help us in our prayer-life. See Genesis 17:2;
Exodus 6:6; Genesis 22:14.

For them that honour Me I will honour.

1 S A M U E L   2 : 3 0

To believe that the Lord will hear my prayer is honor to His truthfulness. He has said that He will, and I believe that He will keep His word. It is honorable to His power. I believe that He can make the word of His mouth stand fast and steadfast. It is honorable to His love. The larger things I ask the more do I honor the liberality, grace and love of God in asking such great things. It is honorable to His wisdom; for if I ask what He has told me to ask, and expect Him to answer me, I believe that His word is wise, and may safely be kept. If thou wouldst dishonor every attribute of God, pray with unbelief; but if, on the contrary, thou wouldst put a crown on the head of Him who hath saved thee, and who is the God of thy salvation, believe that if thou askest He will give, and if thou knockest He will open unto thee.

C. H. S P U R G E O N

We are much more likely to ask too little when we pray than we are to ask too much. Honor Him with a large request today.

In Gibeon the Lord appeared to Solomon in a dream by night: and God said, Ask what I shall give thee.

1   K I N G S   3 : 5

Hitherto have ye asked nothing in My name: ask, and ye shall receive, that your joy may be full.

J O H N   1 6 : 2 4

*I*t is well for us that we are commanded to pray, or else in times of heaviness we might give it up. If God command me, unfit as I may be, I will creep to the footstool of grace; and since He says, "Pray without ceasing," though my words fail me and my heart itself will wander, yet I will still stammer out the wishes of my hungering soul and say, "O God, at least teach me to pray and help me to prevail with Thee."

C . H . S P U R G E O N

Satan the Hinderer may build a barrier about us, but he can never roof us in, so that we cannot look up.

J . H U D S O N T A Y L O R

Since our God has opened the way to His throne of grace, and bidden us draw near and ask what He shall give us, let us prize the privilege and ask and receive that we may have fullness of joy.

*I will stand upon my watch, and set me upon the
tower, and will watch to see what He will say unto me.*

HABAKKUK 2:1

*W*hat about the last time we knelt in prayer?
Surely He had more to say to us than we
had to say to Him, and yet we never waited a minute
to see! We did not give Him opportunity for His gracious response. We rushed away from our King's presence as soon as we had said our say, and vaguely
expected Him to send His answers after us somehow
and sometime, but not there and then. What wonder
if they have not yet reached us! The only wonder is that
He ever speaks at all when we act thus. If Mary had
talked to the Lord Jesus all the time she sat at His feet,
she would not have "heard His word." But is not this
pretty much what we have done?

F. R. HAVERGAL

Oh the snare and the sin of hurrying through our
prayer times! How unspeakable is the loss we sustain
because we do not take time to speak fully to the King
and to have Him speak fully to us.

*Therefore to him that knoweth to do good,
and doeth it not, to him it is sin.*

J A M E S   4 : 1 7

*And when the people complained,
it displeased the Lord.*

N U M B E R S   1 1 : 1

*A*ll prayer which has ever brought down blessing has prevailed by the same law of success—the inward impulse of God's Holy Spirit. If, therefore, that Spirit's teachings be disregarded or disobeyed, or His inward movings be hindered, in just such measure will prayer become formal, or be altogether abandoned. Sin, consciously indulged, or duty, knowingly neglected, makes supplication an offence to God.

A .   T .   P I E R S O N
I N   *G E O R G E   M Ü L L E R   O F   B R I S T O L .*

Disobedience in any form, a murmuring spirit, hesitancy to enter a pathway or duty divinely opened—all these grieve the Holy Spirit and effectually hinder our prayers. Everything indeed that comes into our lives with which the Holy Spirit has no sympathy is a hindrance to our prayers, and we can have no real liberty until the evil is definitely renounced.

*Peter went up upon the housetop to pray
about the sixth hour.*

A C T S   1 0 : 9

Cornelius . . . prayed to God always.

A C T S   1 0 : 2

*P*ut public or social worship in the place of secret prayer, and you will find, I venture to say, that your individual insight into sin, and righteousness, and judgment, on the one hand, and into Christ your righteousness and sanctification and redemption, on the other is waning, and growing dim, and as it were generalizing itself away into mist and cold. You will find in short that as an individual sinner, an individual believer, you cannot minimize your solitary, secret, individual seasons of confession, petition and praise, without the results that are to be expected. Your spiritual life-pulse will be feebler. Your whole renewed nature and its work will suffer from the center.

H. C. G. M O U L E

Secret prayer is to all other prayer what the rivulets are to a great river itself. When the rivulets fail the river is low; when secret prayer is neglected other prayer loses its power.

Grow in grace, and in the knowledge of
our Lord and Saviour Jesus Christ.
2   P E T E R   3 : 1 8

And the apostles said unto
the Lord, Increase our faith.
L U K E   1 7 : 5

*D*o not expect, when you trust Christ to bring you into a new, healthy prayer-life, that you will be able all at once to pray as easily and powerfully and joyfully as you fain would. But just bow quietly before God in your ignorance and weakness. That is the best and truest prayer, to put yourself before God just as you are. "We know not what to pray as we ought"; ignorance, difficulty, struggle marks our prayer all along. But, "the Spirit Himself, helpeth our infirmities." How? "The Spirit" deeper down than our thoughts or feelings "maketh intercession for us with groanings which cannot be uttered."

A N D R E W   M U R R A Y

There should be a progressive development of the prayer-life of the Christian through all his days. Prayer should become more and more a fruitful exercise to the soul.

And as He prayed, the fashion of His countenance was altered, and His raiment was white and glistering.

L U K E   9 : 2 9

*I*t is a very interesting fact that it was as Jesus was praying that He was transfigured. When He first knelt on the cold mountain there was no brightness in His face. But, as He continued in prayer, there began to be, at length, a strange glow on His features. Brighter and brighter it grew, until His face shone as the sun. Heaven came down to earth, and glory crowned the transfiguration mount.

What was true for Him in His human life is true also for His people. Prayer transfigures. There may be no bodily transfiguration as there was in the case of Jesus. Yet we have all seen human faces which had a strange light in them, caused by the peace and joy within.

J . R . M I L L E R

How quickly prayer transforms the weary worn countenance and imparts to it sweetest restfulness and calm! How constantly prayer keeps transforming the soul into the likeness of Christ. Would you become more like Christ, be more with Him in prayer.

O Lord God of Abraham, Isaac, and of Israel,
our fathers, keep this forever in the imagination of
the thoughts of the heart of Thy people, and
prepare their heart unto Thee.

1 C H R O N I C L E S 2 9 : 1 8

We ought not to need, when the prayer time comes, to do all the work of preparation then. But on the other hand, when the time does come, we shall always gain by a first earnest and concentrating act of recollection . . . in the Lord's presence; by a solemn re-stating to ourselves of Who He is to whom we are about to speak, of what He is to us and we to Him. . . . Not very many years ago it was a common thing, in pious households, as the hour of evening family prayer approached, for each person to retire apart for a short season of private prayer. Let our souls so retire, and so recollect, before we enter the immediate precincts of the secret throne of grace.

H. C. G. MOULE

Oh the pure delight of a single hour
That before Thy throne I spend,
When I kneel in prayer, and with Thee my God,
I commune as friend with Friend.

Let all bitterness, and wrath, and anger,
and clamour, and evil speaking be put away from
you, with all malice: And be ye kind one to another,
tenderhearted, forgiving one another, even as
God for Christ's sake hath forgiven you.

E P H E S I A N S 4 : 3 1 , 3 2

*T*he prayer must wait for its answer until some wrong is taken out of the way. The wrong feeling toward a brother man, the quarrel the bitterness of which remains, the transaction which we are not willing to review calmly because we are afraid we may have to say that there is sin in it, the plea whereby we justify conformity to the world—are all to be considered when we stand waiting for the answer that does not come. We are made to ask whether the cause is not in something we have done or not done. It will not take a large sin. A small bit of iron will disturb the magnetic needle. A small grain of sand will grate harshly in the delicate mechanism of the eye.

D. W. FAUNCE

The vessels must be clean into which God would pour His richest blessings.

Trust in Him at all times; ye people, pour out your heart before Him: God is a refuge for us.

PSALM 62:8

I have drunk neither wine nor strong drink, but have poured out my soul before the Lord.

1 SAMUEL 1:15

Ye to whom His love is revealed, reveal yourselves to Him. His heart is set on you, lay bare your hearts to Him. Turn the vessel of your soul upside down in His secret presence, and let your inmost thoughts, desires, sorrows, and sins be poured out like water. Hide nothing from Him, for you can hide nothing. To the Lord unburden your soul; let Him be your only father-confessor, for He only can absolve you when He has heard your confession. To keep our griefs is to hoard up wretchedness. The stream will swell and rage if you dam it up: give it a clear course, and it leaps along and creates no alarm.

C. H. SPURGEON

Prayer becomes very real when it is like pent-up steam that must find vent. When the "subdued sighings of the soul" begin to find expression prayer becomes a pouring out of the heart.

*But the thing displeased Samuel,
when they said, Give us a king to judge us.
And Samuel prayed unto the Lord.*

1   S A M U E L   8 : 6

*S*amuel turned toward the elders of Israel, heard their story, then turned his face about and told God concerning the whole thing. It is a wonderful kind of life—God always so nigh at hand. Will He not be equally nigh at hand today? Is He still to be sought for as if He had hidden Himself beyond the voice of the thunder, or is He nigh at hand so that a sigh can reach Him, and a whisper can stir His omnipotence into beneficent interposition on behalf of His sorrowing, suffering people? It would be a new life to us if we knew that God beset us behind and before, laid his hand upon us, and that not a throb of our heart escaped the care of His love!

JOSEPH PARKER

Are we meeting the great emergencies of our life in prayer, and are we in the light which God gives, finding blessed solutions to life's problems?

Whosoever shall call upon the name
of the Lord shall be saved.
R O M A N S 1 0 : 1 3

Call ye upon Him while He is near.
I S A I A H 5 5 : 6

*W*hen we enter a store or shop we ask the salesman to hand us the particular article we want. There is an enormous amount of pointless, prayerless praying done in our devotional meetings; it begins with nothing and ends nowhere. The model prayers mentioned in the Bible were short and right to the mark. "God be merciful to me a sinner." "Lord save me," cries sinking Peter. "Come down ere my child die," exclaims the heart-stricken nobleman. Old Rowland Hill used to say, "I like short ejaculatory prayer; it reaches heaven before the devil can get a shot at it."

T H E O D O R E L. C U Y L E R

No matter where we are we can make connections with the Central Office in the Heavenlies, and with the rapidity of electricity call and receive an answer. Do not wait for the set time and place but call upon the Lord anywhere, anytime.

Praise ye the Lord: for it is good to sing praises unto our God; for it is pleasant; and praise is comely.

P S A L M   1 4 7 : 1

*P*raise is an important element of prayer. Prayer is more than a recital of our requests, and a recognition of received blessings. Prayer stands, as it were, for communion, or correspondence, between ourselves and our loving Father in heaven. It is the opening of our hearts to Him. If, then, we seem to be thinking only of what we want from Him, or only of what we have had from Him, we are lacking in that which pleases Him most of all—and that is our personal love for Him. We need never fear that we are lacking in the spirit of prayer if we pour out our hearts in loving praise of God, even though we forget for the time to name the special blessings we have had, or would like to have, from Him. God loves to be loved, and He loves to hear us say that we love Him.

It is good to sing praises unto our God, for it brings to the soul that joy and liberty so essential to prayer.

I exhort therefore, that supplications, prayers,
intercessions, be made for all men.
1   T I M O T H Y   2 : 1

*S*top praying so much for yourself; begin to ask unselfish things, and see if God won't give you faith. See how much easier it will be to believe for another than for your own petty self. Try the effect of praying for the world, for definite things, for difficult things, for glorious things, for things that will honor Christ and save mankind, and after you have received a few wonderful answers to prayer in this direction, see if you won't feel stronger to touch your own little burden with a divine faith, and then go back again to the high place of unselfish prayer for others.

A . B . S I M P S O N

Our prayers as a rule are too circumscribed. We do not frequently enough lift up our eyes and look out upon God's great world-field that we may see and pray for its needs. The millions of China and India and Africa should not be lost sight of in our prayer work.

I can of Mine own self do nothing:
as I hear, I judge: and My judgment is just;
because I seek not Mine own will, but the will of the
Father which hath sent me.

JOHN 5:30

hrist's life and work, His suffering and death—it was all prayer, all dependence on God, trust in God, receiving from God, surrender to God. Thy redemption, O believer, is a redemption wrought out by prayer and intercession: thy Christ is a praying Christ: the life He lived for thee, the life He lives in thee is a praying life that delights to wait on God and receive all from Him. To pray in His name is to pray as He prayed. Christ is only our example because He is our Head, our Saviour and our Life. In virtue of His Deity and of His Spirit He can live in us: we can pray in His name, because we abide in Him and He in us.

ANDREW MURRAY

As Christ's life was a praying life, and as He is still a praying Christ, so let our lives be praying lives for His glory.

*But we will give ourselves
continually to prayer.*

A C T S   6 : 4

*And all things, whatsoever ye shall ask
in prayer, believing, ye shall receive.*

M A T T H E W   2 1 : 2 2

There are ministers unlettered,
Not of Earth's great and wise,
Yet mighty and unfettered
Their eagle-prayers arise.
Free of the heavenly storehouse!
For they hold the master-key
That opens all the fullness
Of God's great treasury.
They bring the needs of others
And all things are their own,
For their one grand claim is Jesu's name
Before their Father's throne.

F .   R .   H A V E R G A L

*W*hat ministers of blessing to the church, and
to the world, are the men and women of
God who give themselves continually to prayer, and
who have learned the secret of opening "all the fullness
of God's great treasury" for the salvation and enrich-
ment of souls. What higher privilege could we crave
than to be thus a minister of blessing!

The effectual fervent prayer of a
righteous man availeth much.

J A M E S   5 : 1 6

There are noble Christian workers,
The men of faith and power,
The overcoming wrestlers
Of many a midnight hour;
Prevailing princes with their God,
Who will not be denied,
Who bring down showers of blessing
To swell the rising tide.
The Prince of Darkness quaileth
At their triumphant way,
Their fervent prayer availeth
To sap his subtle sway.

F . R .   H A V E R G A L

*T*here is plenty of room for recruits in the ranks
of these "overcoming wrestlers." Why should
there not be large accessions to their number? These
men who prevail are men of like passions with ourselves, and it is just as possible for us to become men
of power in prayer as for them. Not only should we
seek to be "prevailing princes" ourselves, but we should
do all we can to awaken others to be.

*Again I say unto you, That if two of you shall
agree on earth as touching any thing that they shall
ask, it shall be done for them of My Father
which is in heaven.*

MATTHEW 18:19

hree Christians made an agreement to pray for three prominent men in the community, which was done for several weeks. One evening they were gathered with their pastor for a season of devotion, when these three men successively entered to inquire what they must do to be saved. In that circle of prayer to which they already owed so much, they soon found peace.

One of the great needs of the times is circles of praying men and women in our churches, who will make the salvation of certain persons definite subjects of earnest united prayer, and not cease praying till they are saved. You, dear reader, may start such a circle. Speak to your pastor about it and have the suggestion made that such circles be formed all through the church of which you are a member.

Moreover concerning the stranger . . . if they come and pray in this house; then hear Thou from the heavens.

2   C H R O N I C L E S   6 : 3 2 ,   3 3

Neither pray I for these alone, but for them also which shall believe on Me through their word.

J O H N   1 7 : 2 0

*I*s it to dawn on men that praying for men is as much a duty as the giving of money for their necessities; that the other philanthropies that dignify and adorn our century are to have an addition to their force and number, by a newly used instrumentality, that of prayer? For, if a force at all, it must be of no mean rank among those whereby men are to be moved for the better. Praying for men is equally a duty with setting before them an example of honesty, sobriety, and of every religious virtue. Praying for men is a debt due them, to be paid like other obligations.

D. W. F A U N C E

And when can we cease to pray for men? When will men cease to need the prayers of God's people? When shall we cease to need ourselves the intercessions of others, and of Christ for ourselves?

*Now all these things happened unto them
for examples: and they are written for
our admonition, upon whom the
ends of the world are come.*

1 CORINTHIANS 10:11

*T*he prayer of Solomon for God's protecting and forgiving care for his people; the prayer of Hezekiah for recovery from threatening death; the prayer of the publican in the temple; the prayers of the believers in the house of Mary, John Mark's mother; the prayer of our Lord Himself on different occasions—these are examples of what and how much prayer may mean.

These biblical prayers are examples not only in the sense that they are samples, illustrations, but also in that of being meant for imitation. Primarily from Jesus Himself, yet secondarily, too, from our fellow-men and women recorded in the Scriptures, we may learn much about prayer. If you ever are tempted to doubt whether prayer has any value, then make a list of the prayers recorded in the Bible and study them one by one, and you cannot fail to have a new appreciation of what it means to pray.

FROM *HELPFUL THOUGHTS
FOR QUIET HOURS.*

Thy Kingdom come.

MATTHEW 6 : 10

*A*mong the Jews there has been a saying, "He prays not at all in whose prayers there is no mention of the kingdom of God," but the veil which remaineth untaken away in the reading of the Old Testament has hung like a pall over the living experience of this truth as well. And Jewish blindness finds its parallel in the church's neglect of the voice which for centuries has been pleading, largely in vain, "Pray ye the Lord of the harvest to thrust forth laborers into His harvest." Eighteen long centuries of waiting, during which His kingdom has not come, are alike the evidence and the result of the absence of expressed desire that the King and His kingdom should appear.

ROBERT E. SPEER

The kingdom does not come because God's people do not really want it to come. They do not show that they do, neither by prayer, nor works, neither by giving nor going. In whatever measure the kingdom has come in the past it is due to prayer, and so it will be in the future.

*And God is able to make all grace abound toward
you; that ye, always having all sufficiency in all
things, may abound to every good work.*

2   C O R I N T H I A N S   9 : 8

*G*od's real answers to prayer are often seeming
denials. Beneath the outward request He
hears the voice of the inward desire, and He responds
to the mind of the Spirit rather than to the imperfect
and perhaps mistaken words in which the yearning
seeks expression. Moreover, His infinite wisdom sees
that a larger blessing may be ours only by the with-
holding of the lesser good which we seek; and so all
true prayer trusts Him to give His own answer, not in
our way or time, or even our own expressed desire,
but rather His own unutterable groaning within us
which He can interpret better than we. Monica, mother
of Augustine, pleaded with God that her dissolute son
might not go to Rome, that sink of iniquity; but he was
permitted to go, and thus came into contact with
Ambrose, bishop of Milan, through whom he was
converted. God fulfilled the mother's desire while
denying her request.

A . T . PIERSON
IN *GEORGE MULLER OF BRISTOL*

But they that wait upon the Lord shall renew their strength; they shall mount up with wings as eagles.

ISAIAH 40:31

*T*here are heights in experimental knowledge of the things of God which the eagle's eye of acumen and philosophic thought hath never seen; and there are secret paths which the lion's whelp of reason and judgment hath not as yet learned to travel. God alone can bear us there; but the chariot in which He takes us up, and the fiery steeds with which that chariot is dragged, are prevailing prayers. . . . Prevailing prayer takes the Christian to Carmel, and enables Him to cover heaven with clouds of blessing and earth with floods of mercy. Prevailing prayer bears the Christian aloft to Pisgah and shows him the inheritance reserved; ay, and it elevates him to Tabor and transfigures him till in the likeness of his Lord, as He is, so are we also in this world.

C. H. SPURGEON

Our prayer-life should be a ladder not simply for the ascending and descending of angels of blessing, but for the constant ascending of our own souls into the heights of God.

*Let my prayer be set forth before Thee as incense; and
the lifting up of my hands as the evening sacrifice.*

P S A L M 1 4 1 : 2

s incense is carefully prepared, kindled
with holy fire, and devoutly presented
unto God, so let my prayer be. . . . Whatever form the
psalmist's prayer might take, his one desire was that it
might be acceptable of God. Prayer is sometimes presented without words by the very motions of our bodies: bended knees and lifted hands are the tokens of
earnest expectant prayer. Certainly work, or the lifting
up of the hands in labor, is prayer if it be done in
dependence upon God and for His glory: there is a
hand prayer as well as a heart prayer, and our desire is
that this may be sweet unto the Lord as the sacrifice of
eventide.

C. H. S P U R G E O N

If our prayers are as incense they will ascend to God
with a sweet and acceptable fragrance and will be
pleasing in His sight. They must, however, be prayers
of the heart ascending from fires of intensest love to
God if they are to be as incense.

*Who worketh all things after the
counsel of His own will.*

EPHESIANS 1:11

*If we ask any thing according to
His will, He heareth us.*

1 JOHN 5:14

*T*he human will, exercising itself in prayer, has its abundant freedom in that it is in abundant accord with God's will; and so it is in perfect voluntariness under that will; it is as free to ask as is His will to answer. The strictly logical conclusion is this, that by a divine plan there is place for the prayer of man, exactly as for any other form of human exertion. In the natural world, the divine plan of things, in connection with our freedom, is the basis of all human activity. We can depend on the sun to rise and set, on the procession of the seasons, on the ordination of seed-time and harvest, and therefore we labor. We see that laws are fixed, and therefore we labor, and therefore we pray as well.

D. W. FAUNCE

No lesson in the prayer-life is more important for us to learn than that the chief thing is to be and abide in harmony with the will of God.

And they continued stedfastly
in the apostles' doctrine and fellowship,
and in breaking of bread, and in prayers.

A C T S   2 : 4 2

*I*f prayer was thus the power by which the Primitive Church flourished and triumphed, is it not the one need of the church of our days? Let us learn what ought to be counted axioms in our church work. Heaven is as full of stores of spiritual blessing as it was then. God still delights to give the Holy Spirit to them that ask Him. Our life and work are still as dependent on the direct impartation of Divine power as they were in Pentecostal times. Prayer is still the appointed means for drawing heavenly blessings in power on ourselves and those around us. God still seeks for men and women who will, with all their other work of ministering, specially give themselves to persevering prayer.

A N D R E W   M U R R A Y

There is a great danger of the church prayer-meeting becoming a thing of the past. Talking, discussing, exhorting are taking the place of praying.

Strive together with me in your
prayers to God for me.
R O M A N S   1 5 : 3 0

*P*rayer is measured not by length, but by strength. The divine gauge of the worth of prayer is its pressure on the heart of God. The lock of prayer sometimes goes hard, and calls for strength of purpose. The kingdom of heaven has to be taken by force. There is such a thing as laboring and striving in prayer. Thus Jesus prayed in the garden, and Daniel in Babylon, and Epaphras in Paul's hired house. Such were the prayers offered of old in the catacombs as the torchlight flickered; in alpine caves where Waldenses cowered; on hillsides where the covenanters sheltered under the cliffs. . . . Let us pray, remembering that everything depends on the gracious promise of God, but as if the answer depended on the strength and tenacity of our entreaty.

F. B. MEYER

A revival of earnest striving in prayer for a great out-pouring of the Holy Spirit upon the church is one of the greatest needs of the times.

He shall call upon Me, and I will answer him.
P S A L M   9 1 : 1 5

*In the day of my trouble I will call upon Thee,
for Thou wilt answer me.*
P S A L M   8 6 : 7

*I*t is no doubt true that religious thought and communion with God purify, invigorate, and ennoble the soul; but if when we pray we think only or chiefly of the effect of prayer upon ourselves, instead of thinking of its effect in inducing God to grant us what we pray for, we misapprehend the nature of the act. When your child comes to you hungry or thirsty, and asks for food or drink, the child expects you to do something in answer to his request. He does not suppose that the mere act of asking will satisfy his hunger or quench his thirst; and so when we ask God for spiritual wisdom and strength we are not to imagine that the mere asking will make us wiser and stronger. God teaches us, and God strengthens us in answer to our prayer.

R. W. D A L E

Are you satisfied to go on day after day without receiving definite answers to your prayers?

Now when Daniel knew that the writing was signed,
he went into his house; and his windows being open
in his chamber toward Jerusalem, he kneeled upon his
knees three times a day, and prayed, and gave
thanks before his God, as he did aforetime.

D A N I E L   6 : 1 0

A prayer which a man will die sooner than omit is a good deal more than a form. We hear much in this day of the superiority of the free spirit regarding times and seasons and outward expressions of worship, and regarding a devotion concentrated in specific acts at fixed times. But unless there are such fixed acts, there will be little diffused devotion. It will be evaporated out of, not diffused through, the daily life. It there are no reservoirs, there will be no water in the pipes. The nerves must be knit up into ganglia, if there is to be sensibility through all the body. If a man does not pray at definite times, and that daily, he may talk as he likes about all life being worship, but "any time" will soon come to mean "no time."

A L E X A N D E R   M A C L A R E N

*For Christ is not entered into the holy places
made with hands, which are the figures of the true;
but into heaven itself, now to appear
in the presence of God for us.*

H E B R E W S   9 : 2 4

*F*or us the veil is rent. Jesus entered once into the holy place, and as He passed, the heavy folds were rent in twain from the top to the bottom. Surely no priest that witnessed it could ever forget the moment, when, as the earth trembled beneath the temple floor, the thickly woven veil split and fell back, and disclosed the solemnities on which no eyes but those of the high priest dared to gaze. Surely the most obtuse can read the meaning signified herein by the Holy Ghost. There is no veil between us and God but that which we weave by our own sin or ignorance. We may go into the very secrets of His love. We may behold mysteries hidden from before the foundation of the world.

F. B. M E Y E R

Seeing the way to God is clear and open, let us come to Him freely, joyously, boldly, and in full assurance.

*God be merciful unto us, and bless us; and
cause His face to shine upon us; that Thy way may
be known upon earth, Thy saving health
among all nations.*

P S A L M   6 7 : 1 ,   2

*G*od's blessing is to be sought in prayer in
order that God's people may be a blessing.
We are to receive in order that we may pass on. While
we pray for ourselves, and it is important and necessary that we should, the ultimate purpose of our
prayers should be the salvation of all men. While we
reach out our hand in faith to receive the riches of
God's grace, it is that others also may be enriched
through us. Prayer will soon become stagnant and
powerless for our own soul's good if in our praying we
never think of others. True prayer is unselfish. True
prayer follows the outgoing of God's love, and that
reaches to the ends of the earth. If it is a bad sign to
be always praying for others and never for self, it is an
equally bad sign to be always praying for self and
never for others. Study carefully the sixty-seventh
Psalm and learn its lesson for the prayer-life.

C H A R L E S   A .   C O O K

They that be whole need not a physician,
but they that are sick.

MATTHEW 9 : 1 2

For the Son of Man is come to save
that which was lost.

MATTHEW 1 8 : 1 1

*L*et us take time to consider and realize the need. Each Christless soul going down into outer darkness, perishing of hunger, with bread enough and to spare! Thirty million a year dying without the knowledge of Christ! Our own neighbors and friends, souls entrusted to us, dying without hope! Christians around us living a sickly, feeble, fruitless life! Surely there is need for prayer. Nothing, nothing but prayer to God will help, will avail.

ANDREW MURRAY

Are we praying then for a lost world? Have we prayed today for the millions who have no knowledge of Christ? Are we praying daily for the salvation of some friend or neighbor? If Christ suffered to save men, it is a small thing that we pray to save them. And if we do not pray for their salvation, of what avail will all else be that we do?

But thou hast not called upon Me, O Jacob;
but thou hast been weary of Me, O Israel.

I S A I A H   4 3 : 2 2

*N*othing is a surer gauge of our spiritual state than our prayers. There may be a weariness of the brain which is the reaction of overstrain, and against which it is not wise to struggle. When mind and heart are so overpowered by the fatigues of the body that an inevitable drowsiness closes the eye and restrains the flow of thought, it is better to say, with the great Bengel, as we yield ourselves to sleep, "O Lord, we are on the same terms as yesterday." But this is very different from the perfunctory and hurried devotions which arise from the preoccupation of the mind in things of time and sense, or the alienation of the heart from God by sin. If this lethargy is stealing over thee, beware!

F. B. MEYER

Yes—beware! for when our devotions become hurried and perfunctory they soon become irksome. Yes—beware! for prayerlessness means powerlessness, fruitlessness, worldliness, sinfulness, darkness, death!

Praying in the Holy Ghost.

J U D E   2 0

*I*n the consecrated believer the Holy Spirit is pre-eminently a spirit of prayer. If our whole being is committed to Him, He will occupy every moment in communion and occupy every thing as it comes, and we shall pray it out in our spiritual consciousness before we act it out in our lives. We shall, therefore, find ourselves taking up the burdens of life and praying them out in a wordless prayer which we ourselves often cannot understand, but which is simply the unfolding of His thought and will within us, and which will be followed by the unfolding of His providence concerning us.

A. B. SIMPSON

Lord, fill us with the Spirit, that He dwelling within us may make intercession for us according to the will of God, and be at all times the very spring of our prayer-life. May He not only dictate the petitions but give us that Spirit of humility, and work in us that faith, which are so necessary to acceptable prayer.

And He saw that there was no man,
and wondered that there was no intercessor.

I S A I A H   5 9 : 1 6

*H*ow can our intercourse with the Father, in continual prayer and intercession, become what it ought to be, if we and the world around us are to be blessed? As it appears to me, we must begin by going back to God's Word to study what place God means prayer to have in the life of His child and His church. A fresh sight of what prayer is according to the will of God, of what our prayers can be, through the grace of God, will free us from those feeble defective views, in regard to the absolute necessity of continual prayer, which lie at the root of our failure. As we get an insight into the reasonableness and rightness of this divine appointment, and come under the full conviction of how wonderfully it fits in with God's love, and our own happiness, we shall be freed from the false impression of it being an arbitrary demand. We shall with our whole heart and soul consent to it and rejoice in it, as the one only possible way for the blessing of heaven to come to earth.

A N D R E W   M U R R A Y

*For it is God which worketh in you both
to will and to do of His good pleasure.*

P H I L I P P I A N S   2 : 1 3

*I can do all things through Christ
which strengtheneth me.*

P H I L I P P I A N S   4 : 1 3

*C*an it indeed be that those who have never been able to face, much less to overcome the difficulty can yet become mighty in prayer? Tell me, was it really possible for Jacob to become Israel—a prince who prevailed with God? It was. The things that are impossible with men are possible with God. . . . And will you still doubt whether God is able to make you "strivers with God," princes who prevail with Him? Oh, let us banish all fear, and in faith claim the grace for which we have the Holy Spirit dwelling in us, the grace of supplication, the grace of intercession

A N D R E W   M U R R A Y

We cannot fit ourselves for this ministry of prayer for men. We must be Spirit taught, and Spirit empowered. It is not impossible therefore for us to enter upon this ministry in much power, and thereby effectually serve our generation by the will of God.

For this cause I bow my knees unto the Father
of our Lord Jesus Christ, of whom the whole family in
heaven and earth is named, that He would grant
you, according to the riches of His glory,
to be strengthened with might by
His Spirit in the inner man.

E P H E S I A N S   3 : 1 4 – 1 6

*I*ntercessory prayer is a powerful means of grace
to the praying man. Martyn observes that at
times of inward spiritual dryness and depression he
had often found a delightful revival in the act of praying for others, for their conversion, or sanctification, or
prosperity in the work of the Lord. His dealings with
God for them about these gifts and blessings were for
himself the divinely natural channel of a renewed
insight into his own part and lot in Christ, into Christ
as his own rest and power, into the "perfect freedom"
of an entire yielding of himself to his Master for His
work.

H. C. G. MOULE

Paul's two intercessory prayers in Ephesians 1 and 3
are remarkable in setting forth the believer's privileges
and standing in Christ. As we pray these prayers for
others we shall more fully appropriate them for ourselves.

*Desire the sincere milk of the word,
that ye may grow thereby.*

1 PETER 2:2

*I*f the Bible is the World's Prayer Book, not only in its formulas and examples, but also in its promises and in the truths it gives us, all of which minister to our devotion, then can God do a more kindly service than by refraining to give what we ask, until we make use of His Word in securing what may be called the material of prayer? He may wish to incite diligence in discovering truth. Made to wait, we may be led to ask why the answer delays, and so may come to seek in the Scriptures the larger truth.

A praying man, finding "dryness in prayer," should stop and ask for the reason. It will not do to always expect to feel in the same mood in religious exercises, nor to attribute one's weakness in prayer to God's arbitrary "shutting up of the heavens."

D. W. FAUNCE

The prayer spirit will grow as the Word of God ministers to it. Daily Bible reading is as necessary as daily prayer.

*Because Thy loving kindness is better than life,
my lips shall praise Thee. Thus will I bless Thee while
I live: I will lift up my hands in Thy name.*

PSALM 63:3, 4

The deep desires of this psalmist were occasioned by his seclusion from outward forms of worship, which were to him so intimately related to the inward reality that he felt farther away from God in the wilderness than when he caught glimpses of His face through the power and glory which he saw visibly manifested in the sanctuary. But in his isolation he learns to equate his desert yearnings with his sanctuary contemplations and thus glides from longing to fruition. His devotion, nourished by forms, is seen in the psalm in the very act of passing on to independence of form and so springs break out for him in the desert.

His passion of yearning after God rebukes and shames our faint desires. This man's soul was all on the stretch to grasp and hold God. His very physical frame was affected by his intense longing. If he did not long too much, most men, even those who thirst after God most, long terribly too little.

ALEXANDER MACLAREN

And Samuel spake unto all the house of Israel,
saying, If ye do return unto the Lord with all your
hearts, then put away the strange gods and Ashtaroth
from among you, and prepare your hearts unto
the Lord, and serve Him only.

1   S A M U E L   7 : 3

A Christian may often have very earnest desires for spiritual blessings. But alongside of these there are other desires in his daily life occupying a large place in his interests and affections. The spiritual desires are not all-absorbing. He wonders that his prayer is not heard. It is simply that God wants the whole heart. "The Lord thy God is one Lord, therefore thou shalt love the Lord thy God with all thy heart." The law is unchangeable. God offers Himself, gives Himself away, to the whole-hearted who give themselves wholly away to Him. He always gives us according to our heart's desire. But not as we think it, but as He sees it.

A N D R E W   M U R R A Y

David said, "I entreated thy favor with my whole heart," Psalm 119:58. In no other way should we ever seek God's face.

*But when ye pray, use not vain repetitions
as the heathen do: for they think that they shall be
heard for their much speaking. Be not ye
therefore like unto them.*

M A T T H E W   6 : 7 ,   8

We are apt to feel as if, by our prayers, we laid God under obligations to save us; as if our feeble imperfect services were "profitable to Him." Suppose a poor beggar should say of some rich nobleman, "He is under great obligations to me," and when asked "why?" should answer, "I have been a beggar every day for a great many years, and told him a long story of my wants, and asked him to help me." You can see how absurd this appears; and yet it is precisely similar to our conduct; except indeed the disparity between God and us is infinitely greater than can exist between any two mortals.

E D W A R D   P A Y S O N

The devil will even try to turn our liberty or power in prayer into a snare to our souls, and fill us with self-gratulation, and lead us to think that we are pretty good, and that God ought to bless us because we pray so much.

Let us therefore come boldly unto the throne of grace.

HEBREWS 4:16

O that one might plead for a man with God, as a man pleadeth for his neighbor.

JOB 16:21

*G*eorge Müller stored up reasons for God's intervention. As he came upon promises, authorized declarations of God concerning Himself, names and titles He had chosen to express and reveal His true nature and will, injunctions and invitations which gave to the believer a right to pray and boldness in supplication—as he saw all these, fortified and exemplified by the instances of prevailing prayer, he laid these arguments up in memory, and then on occasions of great need brought them out and spread them before a prayer-hearing God.

A. T. PIERSON
IN *GEORGE MÜLLER IN BRISTOL*

How little we use this method of holy argument in prayer, and yet there are many examples of it in Scripture. Abraham, Jacob, Moses, Elijah, Daniel all used arguments in prayer, and claimed the divine interposition on the ground of the pleas which they presented.

But this I say, He which soweth sparingly
shall reap also sparingly; and he which soweth
bountifully shall reap also bountifully.

2   C O R I N T H I A N S   9 : 6

*N*ow it strikes me that whenever our Lord gives you the special inclination to pray, you should double your diligence. You ought always to pray and not to faint; yet when He gives you the special longing after prayer, and you feel a peculiar aptness and enjoyment in it, you have, over and above the command which is constantly binding, another command which should compel you to cheerful obedience. . . . Our desires to pray should be an indication that the set time to favor Zion has come. Sow plentifully now, for thou canst sow in hope. Plow joyously now, for thy harvest is sure. Wrestle now, Jacob, for thou art about to be made a prevailing prince, and thy name shall be called Israel.

C. H. SPURGEON

If we pray but little the answers to our prayers must necessarily be proportionately small, but if we bring large petitions to our King we shall receive abundantly.

Teach us what we shall say unto Him.
JOB 37:19

*F*rances Ridley Havergal had definite subjects for prayer for each day. Besides special subjects, which were assigned to different days of the week, she wrote out the following general subjects of prayer for each day.

Morning

For the Holy Spirit. Perfect trust all day. Watchfulness. To be kept from sin. That I may please Him. Guidance, growth in grace. That I may do His will. That He would use my mind, lips, pen, all. Blessing and guidance in each engagement and interview of the day.

Evening

For forgiveness and cleansing. Mistakes overruled. Blessing on all said, written, and done. For conformity to His will, and Christ's likeness. That His will may be done in me. For a holy night. Confession. For every one for whom I have been specially asked to pray.

Orderliness, definiteness, fullness of scope should characterize our praying. Some such plan as the above would be a great help to many.

*And the people waited for Zacharias, and
marvelled that he tarried so long in the temple.
And when he came out, he could not speak to them:
and they perceived that he had seen a vision
in the temple: for he beckoned unto
them, and remained speechless.*

L U K E   1 : 2 1 ,   2 2

No prayer is long that is prayed with the heart: as long as the heart can talk, the prayer is very brief—let that be the measure and standard of our long and much praying. . . . Sometimes we can talk the whole day with Him, we cannot tell where the growing numbers of our praise will end, our heart is enlarged in great and free utterance, and then we enter into the mystery of communion; not asking, begging, soliciting, wanting more and more, like the horse-leech, but talking out to Him as the dews go up to the morning sun. . . . A day's long talk, a night's long communion, will be but too short, if you see the King as it were face to face.

J O S E P H   P A R K E R

Blessed is that man who spends more time than usual in prayer because he is kept by new revelations of heavenly things, and new assurances of heavenly blessings.

And Moses did as the Lord commanded him.

LEVITICUS 8:4; NUMBERS 20:27

*So he (Elijah) went, and did according
to the word of the Lord.*

1 KINGS 17:5

*I*t is as men live that they pray. It is the life that
prays. It is the life that, with whole-hearted devotion, gives up all for God and to God, that can claim
all from God. Our God longs exceedingly to prove
Himself the Faithful God and Mighty Helper of His
people. He only waits for hearts wholly turned from
the world to Himself, and open to receive His gifts.
The man who loses all will find all; he dare ask and
take it.

ANDREW MURRAY

It is only when we do as the Lord commands, live
according to His word, that we can command Him in
prayer. Isaiah 45:11. Moses and Elijah and others were
bold in prayer, and wrought mighty things thereby
because they were faithful in obeying God.

This is a condition we should never lose sight of in
our praying. When we pray it is well to ask, "Am I
doing what I know God wants me to do?"

*Call upon Me in the day of trouble:
I will deliver thee, and thou shalt glorify Me.*

PSALM 50:15

*M*en honor God by asking and taking, not by giving. They glorify Him when, by calling on Him in trouble, they are delivered; and then, by thankfulness and service, as well as by the evidence which their experience gives that prayer is not in vain, they again glorify Him. All sacrifices are God's before they are offered, and do not become any more His by being offered. He neither needs nor can partake of material sustenance. But men's hearts are not His without their glad surrender, in the same way as after it; and thankful love, trust and obedience are as the food of God, sacrifices acceptable, well-pleasing to Him.

ALEXANDER MACLAREN

Let us learn to receive much from God that thereby in the richness of the gifts He bestows He may be glorified. Then when we receive His gifts let our best return be our sincerest praise, and our most loving obedience.

*And having an high priest over the house of God; let us
draw near with a true heart in full assurance of faith.*

H E B R E W S   1 0 : 2 1 ,   2 2

I can understand why the Holy Ghost is so careful to tell us again and again that Christ is now
"seated at the right hand of God." It means that He is
in the place of power unquestionably. But it means
more than that; it means that He is in the reception-
room of everlasting mercy, in the audience chamber of
grace and intercession. There He sits forever to receive
the applicants for pardon, to speak in the old familiar
tones of mercy and compassion to those that come
from the east, and from the west, and from the north,
and from the south, to sit down in the kingdom of
God. . . . And it is most significant to me that the writer
of the Epistle to the Hebrews, after saying, "But this
man, after He had offered one sacrifice for sins, forever sat down on the right hand of God," should then
add, "Therefore let us draw near with a true heart, in
full assurance of faith."

A .   J .   G O R D O N

For in that He himself hath suffered being tempted,
He is able to succour them that are tempted.

H E B R E W S 2 : 1 8

*D*o we not need succor? Certainly; and He is able to succor the tempted, because he has suffered the very worst that temptation can do. Not that there was ever one symptom or thought of yielding; yet suffering to the point of extreme anguish beneath the test.

O sufferers, tempted ones, desolate and not comforted, lean your heads against the breast of the God-Man, whose feet have trodden each inch of your thorny path, and whose experiences of the power of evil will qualify Him to strengthen you to stand, to lift you up if you are fallen, to speak such words as will heal the ache of the freshly gaping wound. If He were impassive, and had never wept, or fought in the Garden shadows, or cried out forsaken on the cross, we had not felt Him so near as we can do now in all hours of bitter grief.

F. B. MEYER

How our hearts are drawn to the tender and sympathizing Christ. He will not turn thee away or disappoint thee today. Trust Him.

And when they had prayed, the place
was shaken where they were assembled together;
and they were all filled with the Holy Ghost, and they
spake the word of God with boldness.

A C T S   4 : 3 1

*C*hrist actually meant prayer to be the great power by which His church should do its work, and the neglect of prayer is the great reason the church has not greater power over the masses in Christian and in heathen countries.

Nothing but intense believing prayer can meet the intense spirit of worldliness, of which complaint is everywhere made.

Intercession is the most perfect form of prayer; it is the prayer Christ ever liveth to pray on His throne.

God's giving is inseparably connected with our asking.

ANDREW MURRAY

You and I cannot afford to in any way belittle or neglect that which God has made so great and essential to our own spiritual life, and growth of His kingdom. Oh for a band of men and women who will enter into God's thoughts about prayer and devote themselves to the prayer work of the church.

*Quicken me after Thy loving kindness; so shall
I keep the testimony of Thy mouth.*

P S A L M   1 1 9 : 8 8

*I*f we are revived in our own personal piety we
shall be out of reach of our assailants. Our best
protection from tempters and persecutors is more life.
Loving kindness itself cannot do us greater service
than by making us to have life more abundantly. When
we are quickened we are able to bear affliction, to baf-
fle cunning, and to conquer sin. We look to the loving
kindness of God as the source of spiritual revival, and
we entreat the Lord to quicken, not according to our
deserts, but after the boundless energy of His
grace. . . . We ought greatly to admire the spiritual pru-
dence of the Psalmist, who does not so much pray for
freedom from trial as for renewed life that he may be
supported under it.

When the inner life is vigorous all is well. David
prayed for a sound heart in the closing verse of the last
octave, and here he seeks a renewed heart; this is going
to the root of the matter by seeking that which is the
most needful of all things.

C . H . S P U R G E O N

He hath made us accepted in the beloved.

E P H E S I A N S 1 : 6

*Go up in peace to thine house; see, I have hearkened
to thy voice, and have accepted thy person.*

1 S A M U E L 2 5 : 3 5

*A*s surely as the prayers go up from the accepted one, so surely will the blessings come down. When Esther had touched the golden sceptre, "then said the king unto her, What wilt thou, Queen Esther? and what is thy request? it shall be given thee to the half of the kingdom." But there is no "half" in our King's promise. He says "all things" and "whatsoever." And He does do exceedingly abundantly above all that we ask or think, and more than fulfills our little scanty requests.

F. R. H A V E R G A L

Be sure you are on the ground of acceptance, and then all else will follow. That ground is not in anything we are or do; it is in Christ. Our prayers are accepted not because of their earnestness, or sincerity, but because we are one with Christ, because we abide in Him.

So Hannah rose up, after they had eaten in Shiloh, and after they had drunk. . . . And she was in bitterness of soul, and prayed unto the Lord, and wept sore.

1 S A M U E L   1 : 9 ,   1 0

*L*ooked at in itself, Hannah's prayer was selfish and poor in its spiritual tone; but the woman did not know what she was praying for altogether. It is so with us in our highest devotions. God inspires the prayer, and then answers it, dictates the language, and then satisfies the petition. So those persons who are asking for what may be called a little ordinary daily blessing may, in reality, be asking for a gift the influence of which shall reach through ages, shall palpitate through eternity. Hannah says, Give me a man child! She knows not the destinies that are involved in that prayer.

J O S E P H   P A R K E R

"Now unto Him that is able to do exceeding abundantly above all that we ask or think, according to the power that worketh in us. Unto Him be glory in the church by Jesus Christ, throughout all ages, world without end. Amen."

E P H E S I A N S   3:20,   21

*Verily God hath heard me; He hath attended
to the voice of my prayer.*

PSALM 66:19

I have sought God's aid, and assistance, and
help in all my manifold undertakings, and
though I cannot here tell the story of my private life
in God's work, yet if it were written it would be a
standing proof that there is a God that answers prayer.
He has heard my prayers, not now and then, nor once
nor twice, but so many times, that it has grown into a
habit with me to spread my case before God with the
absolute certainty that whatsoever I ask of God, He
will give to me. . . . In all labor there is profit, but most
of all in the work of intercession: I am sure of this for
I have reaped it.

C. H. SPURGEON

The testimonies of God's servants to the blessedness
and power of prayer should greatly encourage us and
constantly strengthen our faith. When you have
received answers to your prayers be free to speak of it
as David did. Stimulate the prayer-life of your brethren
by telling how God hath attended unto the voice of
your prayer.

*Draw nigh to God, and He
will draw nigh to you.*
J A M E S   4 : 8

It is good for me to draw near to God.
P S A L M   7 3 : 2 8

❋

*C*ould one imagine any exercise more adapted to ennoble man than this of true prayer? It would promote that genuine humility which consists well with the highest exaltation. It lifts mind and heart toward Him who is the sum of all excellence. We grow like Him whom we adore. We are ourselves exalted in exalting Him. It stands to reason that no man can be a worse man, but on the contrary, a better man for entering daily his closet and praying to his Father and his God. Prayer tends to make the relations we sustain to God more definite. It is an act that is between Himself and our central selves. It is called "drawing near to God." The sense of the Divine Being as one ever present may grow dull elsewhere, but it becomes sharp again in the closet.

D. W. FAUNCE

Prayer lifts man into his true place in the universe and properly adjusts him to all things.

God be merciful unto us and bless us; and cause His face to shine upon us. That Thy way may be known upon earth, Thy saving health among all nations.

PSALM 67:1, 2

I will bless thee and thou shalt be a blessing.

GENESIS 12:2

*W*e have thought of our work in preaching or visiting as our real duty, and of prayer as a subordinate means to do this work successfully. Would not the whole position be changed if we regarded the ministry of intercession as the chief thing—getting the blessing and power of God for the souls entrusted to us? Then our work would take its right place and become the subordinate one of really dispensing blessing which we had received from God. It was when the friend at midnight, in answer to his prayer, had received from another as much as he needed, that he could supply his hungry friend.

ANDREW MURRAY

The putting of first things first is one of the most necessary lessons for us to learn in our Christian life. Let us ask God to teach us and help us to put prayer in its proper place.

Hear my voice, O God, in my prayer:
preserve my life from fear of the enemy.

P S A L M   6 4 : 1

e who can cry, "Hear, O God, guard, hide," has already been able to hide in a safe refuge. "The terror caused by the enemy" is already dissipated when the trembling heart grasps at God; and escape from facts which warrant terror will come in good time. This man knows himself to be in danger of his life. There are secret gatherings of his enemies, and he can almost hear their loud voices as they plan his ruin. What can he do in such circumstances but fling himself on God? No thought of resistance has he. He can but pray, but he can pray; and no man is helpless who can look up. However high and closely engirdling may be the walls that men or sorrows build around us, there is always an opening in the dungeon roof, through which heaven is visible and prayers can mount.

A L E X A N D E R   M A C L A R E N

It is with Him that we have to do, on Him alone we have to wait, from Him alone cometh our salvation and our sufficiency.

J .   H U D S O N   T A Y L O R

Brethren, pray for us.

2   T H E S S A L O N I A N S   3 : 1

And pray one for another.

J A M E S   5 : 1 6

*I*f we suppose that the great object of prayer is to soothe or excite the soul by its reflex influence, we shall see no use in praying for other people, unless they are present to hear us pray; and then we shall think more of the immediate effect on their hearts of what we say to God than of the blessings which God will give them in answer to our intercessions.

The habit of praying for others will discipline us to pray for ourselves in a right way; it will train us to believe that blessings come directly from God in answer to our prayers.

R .   W .   D A L E

The fact that others have prayed for us should stimulate us to pray for others. We need others' prayers; others need our prayers. What a help and a blessing God's people may all be to each other through prayer. When they cannot help in any other way they can in this. Said a missionary worker, "The nearest way to the heart of a Chinaman and the heart of a Hindu is by the throne of God."

*They seek Me daily
and delight to know My ways.*

ISAIAH 58:2

None of God's promises are unconditional; and we have no such assets to our credit that we have a right to draw our checks and demand that God shall pay them. The indispensable quality of all right asking is a right spirit toward our heavenly Father. When a soul feels such an entire submissiveness toward God that it delights in seeing Him reign, and His glory advanced, it may fearlessly pour out its desires; for then the desires of God and the desires of that sincere submissive soul will agree. God loves to give to them who love to let Him have His way; they find their happiness in the chime of their own desires with the will of God.

THEODORE L. CUYLER

Do we delight to let God have His own way in our lives, and when we pray do we desire above all things that His will should be done? This is a true test of our sincerity in praying. It is right at this point that our prayers are often switched off and wrecked.

*God forbid that I should sin against the
Lord in ceasing to pray for you.*

1   S A M U E L   1 2 : 2 3

*I pray God your whole spirit and soul
and body be preserved blameless unto the
coming of our Lord Jesus Christ.*

1   T H E S S A L O N I A N S   5 : 2 3

ake your friends, or better still the members of
the church to which you belong, and set yourself systematically to pray for them.

Ask that this person or those persons may have the
enlightenment and expansion of the Spirit, the quickened love and zeal, the vision of God, the profound
sympathy with Christ, which form the true Christian
life. Pray and watch, and as you watch, still pray. And
you will see a miracle, marvelous as the springing of
flowers in April, or the far-off regular rise and setting
of the planets, a miracle proceeding before your eyes,
a plain answer to your prayers, and yet without any
intervention of your voice or hand. You will see the
mysterious power of God at work upon these souls for
which you pray.

R. F. HORTON

*If we confess our sins, He is faithful and just
to forgive us our sins, and to cleanse us
from all unrighteousness.*

1   J O H N   1 : 9

*H*as there been one hard, judging, censori-
ous, supercilious thought of others during
the day? One indulgence of needless, loveless, critical
expression about them? One allowance of mere preju-
dice against them? One remembered act of any kind,
inward or outward, which has broken the laws of holy
Charity? Has there been any difference, or dissension,
with friend or brother, in which we have loved self, and
its claims and rights, perhaps under color of a zeal for
God? Has there been a swelling heat of pride? Has there
been the wretched flutter of vanity? . . . Confess it all,
articulately to the eternal high priest, in the Holiest, at
the Mercy-seat. Remember the blood of sprinkling; rest
on the Covenant of remission and oblivion. But all the
more for this; extenuate nothing; let the essence of the
confession be a total renunciation and repudiation of the
thing confessed.

H. C. G. M O U L E

As you thus confess lay hold of the promise for
cleansing.

Praying always—
with all perseverance.

E P H E S I A N S 6 : 1 8

*J*ust imagine what the result would be if the child of God had only to kneel down and ask, and get, and go away. What unspeakable loss to the spiritual life would ensue. It is in the difficulty and delay that calls for persevering prayer, that the true blessing and blessedness of the heavenly life will be found. We there learn how little we delight in fellowship with God, and how little we have of living faith in Him. We discover how earthly and unspiritual our heart still is, how little we have of God's Holy Spirit. We there are brought to know our own weakness and unworthiness, and to yield to God's spirit, to pray in us, to take our place in Christ Jesus, and abide in Him as our only plea with the Father.

A N D R E W M U R R A Y

Our richest blessings come through the greatest labor. The finest, richest metals are found in places difficult of access. So to obtain heaven's richest favors we shall need to labor earnestly and long in prayer.

*Then they cried unto the Lord in their trouble,
and He saved them out of their distresses.*

PSALM 107:13

*N*ot a prayer till then. While there was any to help below they would not look above. No cries till their hearts were brought down and their hopes were all dead—then they cried, but not before. So many a man offers what he calls prayer when he is in good case and thinks well of himself, but in very deed the only real cry to God is that which is forced out of him by a sense of utter helplessness and misery. We pray best when we are fallen on our faces in utter helplessness. Speedily and willingly He sent relief. They were long before they cried, but He was not long before He saved. They had applied everywhere else before they came to Him, but when they did address themselves to Him, they were welcome at once.

C. H. SPURGEON

Troubles are permitted often to bring men in humble prayer to God. When they have neglected to seek His face He permits trouble to awaken in them a consciousness of their need of Him.

Freely ye have received, freely give.
M A T T H E W   1 0 : 8

I have planted, Apollos watered, but God gave the increase—For we are laborers together with God.
1   C O R I N T H I A N S   3 : 6 ,   9

For the churches in these days to pray, "Thy kingdom come," and then spend more money on jewelry and cigars than in the enterprise of foreign missions looks almost like a solemn farce. God has no blessings for stingy pockets. When I hear requests for prayer for the conversion of a son or daughter, I say to myself, How much is that parent doing to win that child for Christ? The godly wife who makes her daily life attractive to her husband has a right to ask God for the conversion of that husband; she is cooperating with the Holy Spirit, and prepaying her heart's request. God never defaults; but He requires that we prove our faith by our works, and that we never ask for a blessing that we are not ready to labor for, and to make any sacrifice to secure the blessing which our souls desire.

T H E O D O R E L. C U Y L E R

*The Lord is good unto them that wait for Him,
to the soul that seeketh Him. It is good that a man
should both hope and quietly wait for the
salvation of the Lord.*

L A M E N T A T I O N S   3 : 2 5 ,   2 6

*W*ait for God! We are too feverish, too hasty, too impatient. It is a great mistake. Everything comes only to those who can wait. "They that wait on the Lord shall inherit the earth." You may have had what Joseph had when still a lad, a vision of power and usefulness and blessedness. But you cannot realize it in fact. All your plans miscarry. Every door seems shut. The years are passing over you with the depressing sense that you have not wrought any deliverance in the earth. Now turn your heart to God; accept His will; tell Him that you leave to Him the realization of your dream. "Wait on the Lord, and keep His way, and He shall exalt thee to inherit the land; when the wicked are cut off thou shalt see it."

F. B. M E Y E R

God will not be behind time with His work. He will fulfill His promise and carry out His plan.

Abide in Me and I in you. As the branch cannot bear fruit of itself, except it abide in the vine; no more can ye, except ye abide in Me.

J O H N   1 5 : 4

A biding in Christ means a life of converse with Him. To tell Him all; to talk over all anxieties and occurrences with Him; to speak with Him aloud as to a familiar and interested friend; to ask His counsel or advice; to stop to praise, to adore, and utter words of love; to draw heavily upon His resources, as the branch on the sap and life of the vine; to be content to be only a channel, so long as His power and grace are ever flowing through; to be only the bed of a stream hidden from view beneath the hurrying waters, speeding without pausing toward the sea. This is abiding in Christ.

F. B. MEYER

"Draw heavily upon His resources." Prayer does that. Prayer is to the soul what the sap veins are to the vine; it is the channel through which divine life comes into the soul. Let there be much prayer, let there be much intimate converse with Christ, and there will be fullness of His indwelling.

When I remember these things I pour
out my soul in me.

PSALM 42:4

Therefore will I remember Thee from the land of
Jordan, and of the Hermonites, from the hill Mizar.

PSALM 42:6

*T*o recall past joys adds stings to present grief,
but to remember God brings an anodyne for
the smart. The psalmist is far from the sanctuary, but
distance does not hinder thought. This man's faith was
not so dependent on externals that it could not come
close to God while distant from His temple. It had
been so far strengthened by the encouragement of the
refrain that the reflux of sadness at once rouses it to
action. "My soul is cast down . . . therefore let me
remember Thee." With wise resolve he finds in dejec-
tion a reason for nestling closer to God.

ALEXANDER MACLAREN

We may be far away from our accustomed place of
prayer, and painfully miss the quiet and seclusion of
the closet, but we may still hope in God and rejoice in
Him, and be strengthened by the remembrance of His
goodness and grace.

And her adversary also provoked her sore,
for to make her fret.

1   S A M U E L   1 : 6

*H*annah was in bitterness of soul and wept sore. What use did she make of this daily torment? Do not let us fix upon the one particular thing she had in view, or the one special difficulty that annoyed and perplexed her, but get into the principle of the case. What was the use she made of this daily torment? It was a religious use. She prayed unto the Lord; she rose up and went forward that she might pray mightily before God; she spake in her heart and she poured out her soul before God. That was conquest—that was victory! There is a possibility of having a daily annoyance, and yet turning that daily annoyance into an occasion of nearer and nearer approach to God. Let us then endeavor to turn all our household griefs, family torments, into occasions of profound worship and loving homage to God.

JOSEPH PARKER

> Nearer my God to Thee
> Nearer to Thee!
> E'en though it be a cross
> That raiseth me.
> Nearer to Thee!

Peter therefore was kept in the prison, but prayer was made earnestly of the church unto God for him.

ACTS 12:5

*T*hat prayer availed much: Peter was delivered. . . . The whole power of the Roman Empire, as represented by Herod, was impotent in the presence of the power the church of the Holy Spirit wielded in prayer. They stood in such close and living communication with their Lord in heaven; they knew so well that the words, "all power is given unto Me," and "Lo, I am with you alway," were absolutely true; they had such faith in His promises to hear them whatever they asked; they prayed in the assurance that the powers of heaven could work on earth, and would work at their request, and on their behalf. The Pentecostal Church believed in prayer and practiced it.

ANDREW MURRAY

Let us pray most earnestly for a revival of belief in prayer, and that a spirit of prayer may be poured out upon the whole Church of Christ. "Ye that are the Lord's remembrancers, take ye no rest, and give Him no rest till he establish, and till He make Jerusalem a praise in the earth." Isaiah 62:6, 7.

*Beloved, if our heart condemn us not, we have
boldness toward God, and whatsoever we ask we receive
of Him, because we keep His commandments, and
do the things that are pleasing in His sight.*

1   J O H N   3 : 2 1 ,   2 2   R . V .

*A*ll lack of power to pray aright and perseveringly, all lack of power in prayer with
God, points to some lack in the Christian life. It is as
we learn to live the life that pleases God, that God will
give what we ask. Let us learn from the Lord Jesus, in
the parable of the vine, what the healthy, vigorous life
is that may ask and receive what it will. Hear His voice,
"If ye abide in Me, and My words abide in you, ye
shall ask what ye will, and it shall be done unto you."
And again at the close of the parable, "Ye did not
choose Me, but I chose you, and appointed you, that
you should go and bear fruit, and that your fruit
should abide; that whatsoever ye shall ask the Father
in My Name, He may give it you."

A N D R E W   M U R R A Y

Use "lack of power in prayer" as a probe to find out
where the lack is in the Christian life.

And grieve not the Holy Spirit of God, whereby
ye are sealed unto the day of redemption.

E P H E S I A N S   4 : 3 0

*W*hen men say that they cannot believe, it is probably because they are harboring some evil thing in their hearts, or are conscious of some unrepaired wrong in their lives. These must be dealt with. There must be the righting, so far as possible of ancient injuries; the restitution of ill-gotten gains; the seeking of forgiveness; the adjustment of wrong. The fixed purpose to do this, when an opportunity presents itself, will be sufficient to remove the stumbling-block of faith, which will gush out with the sparkle and song of an imprisoned brook. The inability to realize acceptance with God very often points to something that is grieving the Spirit, and at such times the searching ministry of probing and testing and demolition is invaluable.

F. B. MEYER

What various hindrances we meet,
In coming to a Mercy-seat;
Yet who but knows the worth of prayer,
But wishes to be often there.

But we will give ourselves
continually to prayer.
A C T S   6 : 4

*A*ll labor, bodily or mental, needs time and
effort: we must give ourselves to it.
Nature discovers her secrets and yields her treasures
only to diligent and thoughtful labor. However little we
understand it, in the spiritual husbandry it is the same:
the seed we sow in the soil of heaven, the efforts we
put forth, and the influence we seek to exert in the
world above, need our whole being: we must give ourselves to prayer. But let us hold fast the great confidence that in due season we shall reap, if we faint not.

A N D R E W   M U R R A Y

The pressure of life in our day is such that there is
great danger of prayer being crowded into a very nar-
row corner. We must plan to give time and attention
to the prayer-life as we would for anything else that has
to be done.

J. Hudson Taylor says, "If we are simply to pray to
the extent of a pleasant and enjoyable exercise, and
know nothing of watching and weariness in prayer, we
shall not receive all the blessing that we may."

*Pull me out of the net that they have laid
privily for me: for Thou art my strength.*

P S A L M   3 1 : 4

"For Thou art my strength." What an inexpressible sweetness is to be found in these words! How joyfully may we enter upon labors, and how cheerfully may we endure sufferings when we can lay hold upon celestial power. Divine power will rend asunder all the toils of the foe, confound their politics, frustrate their knavish tricks; he is a happy man who has such matchless might engaged upon his side. Our own strength would be of little service when embarrassed in the nets of base cunning, but the Lord's strength is ever available: we have but to invoke it, and we shall find it near at hand. If by faith we are depending alone upon the strength of the strong God of Israel, we may use our holy reliance as a plea in supplication.

C. H. SPURGEON

Canst thou make the language of Isaiah 12:2 thine own? If thou canst, then thou hast no need to fear what man can do unto thee.

Dearly beloved, avenge not yourselves, but rather give place unto wrath: for it is written, Vengeance is Mine; I will repay, saith the Lord.

ROMANS 12:19

Pray for them which despitefully use you, and persecute you.

MATTHEW 5:44

*T*here will come hours in all our lives when we shall be misconstrued, misunderstood, slandered, falsely accused, wrongfully persecuted. At such times it is very difficult not to act on the policy of the men around us in the world. They at once appeal to law and force and public opinion. But the believer takes his case into a higher court, and lays it before his God. He is prepared to use any means that may appear divinely suggested. But he relies much more on the divine clearing than he does on his own most perfect arrangements. He is content to wait for months and years, till God arise to avenge his cause.

F. B. MEYER

When we sincerely and lovingly pray for our enemies, and trustfully and calmly commit our case to God, we have reached a deep spirituality in our prayer-life.

*And Moses went out from Pharaoh,
and entreated the Lord.*

E X O D U S   8 : 3 0

And Moses cried unto the Lord.

E X O D U S   1 7 : 4

And Moses returned unto the Lord.

E X O D U S   3 2 : 3 1 .

S E E   A L S O   E X O D U S   3 3 : 1 1

*T*he man who led his people to salvation, and through whom the deliverances at the sea and in the wilderness were wrought, was himself a praying man. He lived and walked and talked with God as a friend. In that march, more celebrated than any other in history, in which he led an undisciplined horde through unparalleled difficulties to a splendid success, at every turn he called upon God. Next after our Lord's intercessory prayer for His disciples, the grandest instance of that kind of petition the world ever saw came from the heart and lip of this man Moses. Every miracle of his is born in prayer. He is clearly the greatest genius of his time, and yet in nothing more remarkable than in what, if one may reverently say it, may be called the genius for prayer.

D . W . F A U N C E

How the world needs men today who shall be remarkable for the genius for prayer.

And I looked, and there was none to help;
and I wondered that there was none to uphold.

ISAIAH 63 : 5

*T*hough God had His appointed servants in Israel, watchmen set by Himself to cry to Him day and night and give Him no rest, He often had to wonder and complain that there was no intercessor, none to stir himself up to take hold of His strength. And He still waits and wonders in our day that there are not more intercessors, that all His children do not give themselves to this highest and holiest work, that many who do so, do not engage in it more intensely and perseveringly. He wonders to find ministers of His gospel complaining that their duties do not allow them to find time for this, which He counts their first, their highest, their most delightful, their alone effective work.

ANDREW MURRAY

But when ministers realize that there is no duty so imperative, so pressing, so divinely obligatory as this, they will take time from other things and give to this.

And supplication for all saints.
E P H E S I A N S   6 : 1 8

*T*he duty of praying for others is frequently inculcated in the New Testament. It is one of the obligations arising from that great law which makes it impossible for any of us to live an independent and an isolated life. We are members of one body; if one member suffers, all the members suffer with it; if one member is strong and healthy, all the members share the health and strength. We are not fighting a solitary battle. We belong to a great army, and the fortunes of a regiment in a remote part of the field may give us an easy victory or increase the chances of our defeat. We are to offer supplication for "all the saints." Paul himself asked for the intercessions of the Ephesian Christians. He knew that their prayers might secure for him a clearness and a vigor of thought and a fearlessness of spirit which apart from their prayers he might not possess, and we cannot tell how much of his energy, fire, and courage came to him in answer to the prayers of unknown and forgotten saints.

R . W . D A L E

Do good in thy good pleasure unto Zion:
build thou the wall of Jerusalem.

P S A L M   5 1 : 1 8

s the devout Jew prayed much for his loved Zion, that peace might be within her walls, and prosperity within her palaces, so should every true believer most earnestly pray for the church of Christ. The church has a special claim upon our prayers. Through its prayers we have been blessed, through its ministry we have been saved. We should pray for the purity of the church, that it may be delivered from a worldly spirit, and be wholly separated unto God. That the power of the Holy Spirit may be in its midst continually working mighty signs and wonders. That through its preaching and teaching many souls may be saved, and that those who have been brought to Christ and have united with the church may be established and built up in the truth, and become consecrated Christians. Pray for pastors, deacons, trustees. Pray for the financial needs of the church. Organize a circle of prayer in which the church shall be the special object.

C H A R L E S   A . C O O K

*Open Thou mine eyes, that I may behold
wondrous things out of Thy law.*

P S A L M 1 1 9 : 1 8

---

*T*he prayer implies a conscious darkness, a dimness of spiritual vision, a powerlessness to remove that defect, and a full assurance that God can remove it. It shows also that the writer knew that there were vast treasures in the Word which he had not yet fully seen, marvels which he had not yet fully seen, marvels which we had not yet beheld, mysteries which he had scarcely believed. The Scriptures teem with marvels; the Bible is wonder-land: it not only relates miracles, but it is itself a world of wonders. Yet what are these to closed eyes? And what man can open his own eye since he is born blind? God Himself must reveal revelation to each heart. Scripture needs opening but not half so much as our eyes do; the veil is not on the book, but on our hearts.

C. H. SPURGEON

How much the sustenance of our prayer-life depends upon the answer to the prayer of our text for today. They who have been greatest in prayer have known God's Word most thoroughly. Knowledge helps prayer—and prayer helps knowledge.

And, behold, I send the promise of my Father upon you: but tarry ye in the city of Jerusalem, until ye be endued with power from on high.

LUKE 24 : 49

These all continued with one accord in prayer.

ACTS 1 : 14

*G*od's promises are given not to restrain, but to incite to prayer. They show the direction in which we may ask, and the extent to which we may expect an answer. They are the signed check, made payable to order, which we must endorse and present for payment. Though the Bible be crowded with golden promises from board to board, yet will they be inoperative until we turn them into prayer. It is not our province to argue the reasonableness of this; it is enough to accentuate and enforce it.

F. B. MEYER

The promise of the Spirit constrained the disciples to pray. Are we making as much as we might of the sure things which God has purposed shall be, as incentives to earnest, persevering prayer? He has purposed that His gospel shall be preached throughout the world; are we praying that it may be? God's certainties should inspire prayer.

The Lord of hosts hath sworn, saying, Surely
as I have thought, so shall it come to pass: and as
I have purposed, so shall it stand.

I S A I A H   1 4 : 2 4

*G*od does more than to give general assurance of a willingness to hear prayer, and to relieve human want. He makes mention of specific blessings, which He is ready to bestow. These more minute pledges are in various forms of promise, prophecy, covenant, and command. A promise is a direct engagement; a covenant is a still more formal and solemn act, usually accompanied by a seal; a prophecy is a statement of divine purpose, intended for our encouragement in prayer and labor; and a command implies a result which God is willing to aid us in securing. It is only necessary, then, to ascertain that the desired favor is covered by some promise, covenant, prophecy, or command, to have a perfect warrant for faith that in answer to prayer God will bestow that very thing.

W I L L I A M   W .   P A T T O N

A careful use of the suggestion given above cannot fail to help our faith as we pray. Ask—Has God covered this prayer with a pledge?

*And whatsoever ye shall ask in My name, that will I
do, that the Father may be glorified in the Son.*

JOHN   14 : 13

o ask in Jesus' name is to ask by virtue of your
unity with Him. The name represents the person, as my name represents me, and your name represents you. What differentiates us from each other is
the name, because the name represents the nature, the
personality. "Whatsoever ye shall ask the Father, by
virtue of your union with Me, shall be done you," and
six times in this one discourse that promise is given.
And it is a new lesson; for Christ says, "Hitherto ye
have asked nothing in My name." No one in Old
Testament times had asked in His name, and, up to this
point, no disciple of Christ had yet asked in His name,
because the unity of Jesus Christ had never become
sufficiently appreciated so that they understood their
right and privilege of asking by virtue of such identity
with Him.

A. T. PIERSON

Do we sufficiently appreciate our union with Christ to
make it a great help in our prayer-life? Let us seek today
to lay hold of this truth more fully.

*If ye shall ask any thing in
My name, I will do it.*

J O H N   1 4 : 1 4

*T*ake a simple illustration: When I was in Belfast a few years ago I wanted to visit Prang's chromo-lithographic works. A great deal of the process is secret, and strangers are not admitted, and I could not get access to the works. But my friend and host, Robert Corry, Esq., said, "If you would like to go through, I can easily secure you the permission." He took his card and wrote over it: "Will Messrs. Prang and Co. kindly show Dr. and Mrs. Pierson through their works, and oblige Robert Corry." I presented this card, and they detached the foreman of the works, who guided us for two hours, and showed us even the private processes connected with the production of Prang's fine products. Now, observe: I could not have gone through those shops on my own merits, or in my own name; but the name of Robert Corry carried me through. Now, when I presented that card, who made the request? Robert Corry. I presented it, but he made it. While we present the supplication, Christ makes it. It is in His name.

A. T. PIERSON

*Blessed be the Lord, because He hath heard
the voice of my supplications.*

P S A L M   2 8 : 6

They who pray well will praise well; prayer and praise are the two lips of the soul; two bells to ring out sweet and acceptable music in the ears of God; two angels to climb Jacob's ladder; two altars smoking with incense; two of Solomon's lilies dropping a sweet-smelling myrrh; they are two young roes that are twins, feeding upon the mountain of myrrh and the hill of frankincense. . . . Real praise is established upon sufficient and constraining reasons; it is not irrational emotion, but rises, like a pure spring, from the deeps of experience. Answered prayers should be acknowledged. Do we not often fail in this duty? Would it not greatly encourage others, and strengthen ourselves, if we faithfully recorded divine goodness, and made it a point of extolling it with our tongue? God's mercy is not such an inconsiderable thing that we may safely venture to receive it without so much as thanks. We should shun ingratitude, and live daily in the heavenly atmosphere of thankful love.

C . H . S P U R G E O N

*Where the Spirit of the Lord
is, there is liberty.*

2 CORINTHIANS 3:17

There are breathings of God from the highest heavens. They incite in us corresponding breathings of desire to pray. They come to us in the midst of our work, while we walk in the street, and in the waking hour of the night. There are instant petitions that spring to our lips, and they will alter themselves. The prayer prays itself. It is hardly ours, for it is not born of self, not offered by act of will. We cannot stop work to go to the closet, nor wait to bow the reverent knee. These "breathings of desire" come on weekdays as well as on Sundays. Then it is a joy to pray, a relief to pray.

D. W. FAUNCE

There is all the difference between prayer which springs forth like water form an artesian well, and prayer which has to be brought forth with effort like water from a faulty pump. Oh, for liberty and spontaneity in prayer! This liberty is possible, however, only when the Holy Spirit floods the soul with prayer and lifts the soul into communion with God.

I cried to Thee, O Lord; and unto the Lord,
I made supplication.

P S A L M   3 0 : 8

*P*rayer is the unfailing resource of God's
people. If they are driven to their wits' end,
they may still go to the mercy seat. When an earthquake makes our mountain tremble, the throne of
grace still stands firm, and we may come to it. Let us
never forget to pray, and let us never doubt the success
of prayer. The hand that wounds can heal; let us turn
to Him who smites us, and He will be entreated of us.
Prayer is better solace than Caius building a city, or
Saul's seeking for music. Mirth and carnal amusements are a sorry prescription for a mind distracted
and despairing: prayer will succeed where all else fails.

C. H. SPURGEON

What a friend we have in Jesus.
All our sins and griefs to bear!
What a privilege to carry
Everything to God in prayer!

Oh, what peace we often forfeit,
Oh, what needless pain we bear,
All because we do not carry
Everything to God in prayer.

*Who, when they were come down, prayed for them,
that they might receive the Holy Ghost.*

A C T S   8 : 1 5

s this is the only way for an individual to obtain spiritual power, so it is the only way for churches. Prayer, prayer, all prayer—mighty, importunate, repeated, united prayer; the rich and the poor, the learned and the unlearned, the fathers and the children, the pastors and the people, the gifted and the simple, all uniting to cry to God above, that He would come and affect them as in the days of the right hand of the Most High, and imbue them with the Spirit of Christ, and warm them, and kindle them, and make them as a flame of fire, and lay His right hand mightily on the sinners that surround them, and turn them in truth to Him. Such united and repeated supplications will assuredly accomplish their end, and "the power of God" descending will make every such company as a band of giants refreshed with new wine.

WILLIAM ARTHUR

Many a believer might call together a circle of his brethren and sisters to pray thus for the fullness of the Holy Ghost.

*Wherefore in all things it behooved Him
to be made like unto His brethren, that He might
be a merciful and faithful High Priest in
things pertaining to God.*

HEBREWS 2 : 17

*P*rayers prompted by love and in harmony with godly fear are never lost. We may ask for things which it would be unwise and unkind of God to grant, but in that case, His goodness shows itself rather in the refusal than the assent. And yet the prayer is heard and answered. Strength is instilled into the fainting heart. The faithful and merciful High Priest does for us what the angel essayed to do for Him, but how much better, since He has learnt so much of the art of comfort in the school of suffering! And out of it the way finally emerges into life, though we have felt we have left the right hand and foot in the grave behind us. We also discover that we have learnt the art of becoming channels of eternal salvation to those around us.

F. B. MEYER

We need to guard constantly against the temptation to think that our prayers are in vain. The accumulation of prayer may mean a larger blessing at last. See Acts 10:4.

My cup runneth over.
P S A L M   2 3 : 5

Ye are straitened in your own affections.
2   C O R I N T H I A N S   6 : 1 2 , R .   V .

We all know the difference between a man whose profits are just enough to maintain his family and keep up his business, and another whose income enables him to extend the business and help others. There may be an earnest Christian life in which there is prayer enough to keep us from going back, and just maintain the position we have attained to, without much growth in spirituality or Christlikeness. The attitude is more defensive, seeking to ward off temptation, than aggressive, reaching out after higher attainment. If there is indeed to be a going from strength to strength, with some large experience of God's power to sanctify ourselves and to bring down rich blessing on others, there must be more definite and persevering prayer.

A N D R E W   M U R R A Y

Running over, or straitened—which? Barely enough for personal needs, or drawing supplies for others? Our prayer-life fails of its highest end if through it others are not blessed.

For my thoughts are not your thoughts, neither are your ways my ways, saith the Lord. For as the heavens are higher than the earth, so are my ways higher than your ways, and my thoughts than your thoughts.

ISAIAH 55:8, 9

What is the limit of our prayer? This: "Not my will, but Thine, be done!" Is that a limit?—it is glorious liberty! Not my will, but Thine—not a little will, but a great will—not my thought but Thine—not my love, but Thine! Is that a limit? It is the lark rising from its field-nest into the boundless liberty of the firmament! Truly we do not limit ourselves when we exchange the creature for the Creator. When we take up our little thought and say, "Lord, this is what we want—but not our will but Thine be done," do we then throw away the greater for the less? It is a contrast but only such a contrast as you find in earth and heaven, in the blazing sun and the misty night.

JOSEPH PARKER

How mistaken men are in their view about the will of God when they think it means limitation instead of fullness.

For through Him we both have access
by one spirit unto the Father.
E P H E S I A N S   2 : 1 8

*W*e all admit the place the Father and the Son have in our prayer. It is to the Father we pray, and from whom we expect the answer. It is the merit, and name, and life of the Son, abiding in Him and He in us that we trust to be heard. But have we understood that in the Holy Trinity all the Three Persons have an equal place in prayer, and that the faith in the Holy Spirit of intercession as praying in us is as indispensable as the faith in the Father and the Son? How clearly we have this in the words, "Through Christ we have access by one Spirit to the Father."

A N D R E W   M U R R A Y

How small a part, after all, ours seems to be in this prayer work, and yet if our little link of participation is left out the blessing will fail to come. There may be plenty of power generated in the power-house, and the current may be coursing along the wire, but the car will not move until the motorman does his part.

*Let my prayer be set forth
before Thee as incense.*
P S A L M   1 4 1 : 2

*T*here was a fitness in the nature of things in incense being regarded as an embodied prayer. Perfume is the breath of flowers, the sweetest expression of their inmost being, an exhalation of their very life. It is a sign of perfect purity, health and vigor; it is a symptom of full and joyous existence; for disease, and decay, and death yield not pleasant but revolting odors. And, as such, fragrance is in nature what prayer is in the human world. Prayer is the breath of life, the expression of the soul's best, holiest, and heavenliest aspirations; the symptom and token of its spiritual health, and right and happy relations with God.

H U G H   M A C M I L L A N

Incense is not produced by the color or form of the flower but by the very essence of it; so prayer is more than words and sentences; it is the very essence of the inner life pressed out in feeling and desire that ascend to God as incense. Well may we pray. "Let my prayer be set forth before Thee as incense."

Finally, brethren, pray for us,
that the word of the Lord may have free course,
and be glorified, even as it is with you.

2 THESSALONIANS 3 : 1

*P*aul made much of prayer. He was himself a man of prayer, and not only prayed much for his brethren (Romans 1:9, 10:1; Ephesians 1:16, 3:14; Philippians 1:4) but enlisted the prayers of others on his own behalf, and on behalf of the general interests of God's work. He attributed personal blessings and success in the work to the prayers of God's people (Philippians 1:19; 2 Corinthians 1:11).

What a wide field there is to be occupied by prayer workers! Preaching must necessarily be limited, but who can put a limit to the possibilities and power of prayer? The prayer laborer can minister unto the ends of the earth. Missions, missionaries, the heathen, churches in heathen lands, rulers, governments, the nations, the world, the whole Church of Christ, pastors, evangelists, all Christian workers, the coming of Christ, these and a myriad of other subjects may be prayed for.

CHARLES A. COOK

*But we all, with unveiled face reflecting as a mirror
the glory of the Lord, are transformed into the
same image from glory to glory, even as
from the Lord the Spirit.*

2 C O R I N T H I A N S 3 : 1 8

*W*e know not what we should pray for as we
ought"—neither what nor how to pray. But
here is the Spirit's own inspired utterance, and, if the
praying be molded on the model of His teaching, how
can we go astray? Here is our God-given liturgy and
litany—a divine prayer-book. We have here God's
promises, precepts, warnings, and counsels, not to
speak of all the Spirit-inspired literal prayers therein
contained; and, as we reflect upon these, our prayers
take their cast in this matrix. We turn precept and
promise, warning and counsel into supplication, with
the assurance that we cannot be asking anything that
is not according to His will, for are we not turning His
own Word into prayer?

A. T. PIERSON
IN *GEORGE MÜLLER OF BRISTOL.*

Prayer must be divinely inspired, and how can it be
except as the Word of God inspires it by precept and
promise through the Spirit.

He will be very gracious unto thee at the voice of thy cry; when He shall hear it, He will answer thee.

ISAIAH 30:19

*G*od hears prayer—God delights to hear prayer. He has allowed His people a thousand times over to be tried, that they might be compelled to cry to Him, and learn to know Him as the Hearer of Prayer.

Let us confess with shame how little we have believed this wondrous truth, in the sense of receiving it into the heart, and allowing it to possess and control our whole being. That we accept a truth is not enough; the living God, of whom the truth speaks, must in its light so be revealed, that our whole life is spent in His presence, with the consciousness as clear as in a little child toward its earthly parent. I know for certain my Father hears me.

ANDREW MURRAY

How the fact that our God—our Heavenly Father—is indeed the Hearer of Prayer should inspire us to reach out to attain to the very highest development and experiences in our prayer-life. More prayer, greater prayers, larger results should be our constant aim.

Now when I had delivered the evidence
of the purchase, unto Baruch the son of Neriah, I
prayed unto the Lord saying, Ah Lord God!
behold Thou has made the heaven and the earth by
Thy great power and stretched out arm, and
there is nothing too hard for Thee.

JEREMIAH 32:16, 17

There is no help to the troubled soul like that which comes through prayer. You may have no clear vision of God. You may be only able to grope your way in the direction where He sits enshrouded from your view in the thick darkness. You may be able to do little more than recite things which God and you know perfectly well, ending your prayer as Jeremiah did, with the words, "and behold Thou seest it" (v. 24). Nevertheless pray; pray on your knees; "in everything by prayer and supplication . . . let your requests be made known to God," and the peace of God will settle down on and enwrap your weary troubled soul.

F. B. MEYER

Your trouble may be great, the darkness may be dense, the heavens may seem as brass, but ceasing to pray will only make matters worse.

If I regard iniquity in my heart
the Lord will not hear me.

P S A L M 6 6 : 1 8

*I*t does not require what the world pronounces a great sin to break up the serenity of the soul in its devotional hours. The experience of prayer has delicate complications. A little thing, secreted there, may dislocate its mechanism and arrest its movement. The spirit of prayer is to the soul what the eye is to the body—the eye so limpid in its nature, of such fine finish and such intricate convolution in its structure, and of so sensitive nerve, that the point of a needle may excruciate it and make it weep itself away.

Even a doubtful principle of life harbored in the heart is perilous to the peacefulness of devotion.

A U S T I N P H E L P S

Holy living is essential to successful praying.

Who shall ascend into the hill of the Lord?
or who shall stand in His holy place? He that
hath clean hands and a pure heart.

P S A L M 2 4 : 3 , 4

He that turneth away his ear from hearing the law,
even his prayer shall be abomination.

P R O V E R B S 2 8 : 9

Disobedience effectually hinders prayers.

So Joshua did as Moses had said to him, and fought with Amalek: and Moses, Aaron and Hur went up to the top of the hill. And it came to pass when Moses held up his hand, that Israel prevailed.

E X O D U S   1 7 : 1 0 ,   1 1

*M*oses, now eighty-one years old, shrank from the brunt of the battle. He entrusted the troops to Joshua, here first brought into prominence, whilst he climbed the hill, with the sacred rod in his hand. Thence he surveyed the battle and stretched out his hands in prayer—fought with unseen combatants the livelong day, and won the victory by intercessions, of which those steady arms were the symbol. It is a most beautiful picture. Three old men in prayer! Two staying up the third!

In Rephidim we learn the lesson that prayer will do what else were impossible. In earlier days Moses would never have thought of winning a battle but by fighting. He now learns that he can win it by praying.

F. B. MEYER

It takes a long time usually to learn that we can win by praying, but blessed is he who has learned this method of victory.

Be thou for the people to God-ward,
that thou mayest bring the causes unto God.

E X O D U S   1 8 : 1 9

*T*his blessed work of mediatorship was not
borne by Moses as a priest, for as yet the
priesthood was not constituted; but as a large-hearted,
noble man who was at leisure from himself, and had
the ear of God. He was "for the people to God-ward."
And it opens up a very interesting vista of service for
us all, especially for those who are intimate with the
king, and habituated to the royal court. Why should
not we enter more largely into participation with
Moses in this delightful service, which is as open to
those who are slow of speech as to those who are
golden-mouthed, and affords opportunities for the
very powers which most shrink from the glare of pub-
licity and gaze of men?

F. B. MEYER

The church with its Joshuas down in the valley fighting against the Amalekites of iniquity needs men who,
on the mount of prayer, will not fail to hold up holy
hands in intercession until victory is secured. What an
honor to be among the intercessors!

*My voice shalt Thou hear in the morning,
O Lord; in the morning will I direct my prayer
unto Thee, and will look up.*

P S A L M   5 : 3

*S*o fit and useful is morning devotion, it ought not to be omitted without necessity. If our circumstances will allow the privilege, it is a bad sign when no part of the morning is spent in prayer. If God finds no place in our minds at that early and peaceful hour, He will hardly recur to us in the tumults of life. If the benefits of the morning do not soften us, we can hardly expect the heart to melt with gratitude through the day. . . . Let a part of the morning be set apart to devotion; and to this end we should fix the hour of rising, so that we may have an early hour at our disposal.

A U T H O R   U N K N O W N

Happy is the man who gets into touch with God by real fellowship before anything else has an opportunity to engage the attention. Someone has said, we do not need to pray at night, when we are not going to do anything but sleep. But in the morning the difficulties and struggles of life confront us, and we need equipment for the day.

Pray without ceasing.
1 THESSALONIANS 5:17

The Lord will hear when I call unto Him.
PSALM 4:3

*W*e miss very much devotional joy by the neglect of fragmentary prayer. In the intervals which separate periodical seasons of devotion, we need a habit of offering up brief ejaculatory expressions of devout feeling. The morning and the evening sacrifice depend very much upon these interspersed offerings, as these in return are dependent on those. Communion with God in both is assisted by linking the "set times" together by a chain of heavenward thoughts and aspirations, in the breaks which occur in our labors and amusements. Sunrise and sunset may attract our attention more strongly than the succession of golden rays between them, but who can say that they are more cheering?

AUSTIN PHELPS

Life becomes blessed as it is permeated with the spirit of prayer in all its affairs. Prayer should be as natural and as easy as breathing. The prayer-life is best sustained when prayer becomes about as continuous as breathing. Every breath a prayer.

Blessed be the Lord, who daily beareth our burden.

PSALM 68:19, R.V.

Roll thy way upon the Lord.

PSALM 37:5, R.V. MARGIN

*D*o not be satisfied with rolling yourself on God; roll your burden also. He who can carry the one can carry the other. When a tiny boy, trying to help his father move his books, fell on the staircase beneath the weight of a heavy volume, his father ran to his aid and caught up in his arms boy and burden both, and carried them in his arms to his room. And will God deal worse with us? He cannot fail nor forsake. He can smite rocks, and open seas, and unlock the treasures of the air, and ransack the stores of the earth. Birds will bring meat, and fish coins if He bid them. He takes up the isles as a very little thing—how easily, then, your heaviest load: there is nothing so trivial but that you may make it a matter of prayer and faith.

F. B. MEYER

How sweet, my Saviour to repose,
On Thine almighty power!
To feel Thy strength upholding me,
Through every trying hour!

*I will look unto the Lord; I will wait for the
God of my salvation: my God will hear me.*

MICAH 7:7

*T*he power of prayer rests in the faith that God
hears it. In more than one sense this is true.
It is this faith that gives a man courage to pray. It is this
faith that gives him power to prevail with God. The
moment I am assured that God hears me too, I feel
drawn to pray and to persevere in prayer. I feel strong
to claim and to take in faith the answer God gives.
One great reason of lack of prayer is the want of the
living, joyous assurance: my God will hear me.

ANDREW MURRAY

If we have not this assurance let us most earnestly seek
to obtain it—by a renewed study of the Word of God,
by the remembrance of answers to prayer God has
given His people, by reverent consideration of the
character of God, and of all the purposes for which
prayer has been ordained. Let us by no means be satisfied to be without this assurance. By prayer itself let
the soul secure it. The disciples prayed, "Lord, increase
our faith." So may we. Let us look unto the Lord until
assured that He will hear us.

*Thus saith the Lord, the Holy One of Israel,
and His Maker, Ask Me of things to come concerning
My sons, and concerning the work of
My hands command ye Me.*

I S A I A H   4 5 : 1 1

he church, when it is once more a praying Church, will boldly claim of God that He shall stretch forth His hand as the only way to give boldness in preaching His Word. When it is God's "work" we are doing it is our right and privilege not only to ask, but to "command" Him. Faith not only offers a request, but issues a fiat—and says it shall be so. Prayer, says Coleridge, is

> An affirmation and an act,
> That bids eternal truth be fact!

The promise makes prayer bold, for God's Word cannot fail. Fulfillment is as certain as past events are fixed, and the future becomes a present to such faith.

A. T. PIERSON

Timidity, littleness of desire, and smallness of request far too frequently characterize our prayers, where it is our privilege to come to God with boldness, and ask great things from Him.

Elias was a man subject to like passions as we are, and he prayed earnestly that it might not rain: and it rained not on the earth by the space of three years and six months. And he prayed again, and the heaven gave rain, and the earth brought forth her fruit.

J A M E S   5 : 1 7 ,   1 8

*W*hen Elijah was summoned from Zarephath to resume his public work, his marching orders were capped by the specific promise of rain: "Go, show thyself unto Ahab; and I will send rain on the earth." To natural reasons this might have seemed to render prayer unnecessary. Would not God fulfill His promise, and send the rain, altogether irrespective of further prayer? But Elijah's spiritual instincts argued otherwise, and more truly. Though he had never heard the words, yet he anticipated the thought of a late prophet, who, after enunciating all that God was prepared to do for His people, uttered these significant words: "Thus saith the Lord God, I will yet for this be inquired of by the house of Israel, to do it for them."

F. B. M E Y E R

God's promises should stir us to prayer.

*And, behold, I send the promise of my Father
upon you: but tarry ye in the city of Jerusalem,
until ye be endued with power from on high.*

L U K E   2 4 : 4 9

*A*s to the way in which this power may be obtained, we have only to recall the lesson of the Ten Days—"They continued with one accord in prayer and supplication." Prayer earnest, prayer united, and prayer persevering, these are the conditions; and these being fulfilled, we shall assuredly be "endued with power from on high." We should never expect that the power will fall upon us just because we happen once to awake and ask for it. Nor have any community of Christians a right to look for a great manifestation of the Spirit, if they are not ready to join in supplication, and "with one accord," to wait and pray as if it were the concern of each one. The murmurer, who always accounts for barrenness in the church by the faults of others, may be assured that his readiest way to spiritual power, if that be his real object, lies in uniting all, as one heart, to pray without ceasing.

W I L L I A M   A R T H U R

Nevertheless He regarded their affliction,
when He heard their cry: And He remembered
for them His covenant.

PSALM 106:44, 45

All the promises of God in Him are yea, and
in Him Amen, unto the glory of God by us.

2 CORINTHIANS 1:20

Unanswered yet, the prayer your lips have pleaded
In agony of heart these many years?
Does faith begin to fail, is hope declining,
And think you all in vain those falling tears?
Say not the Father has not heard your prayer,
You shall have your desire, sometime, somewhere!

Unanswered yet—though when you first presented
This one petition at the Father's throne
It seemed you could not wait the time of asking,
So anxious was your heart to have it done?
If years have passed since then, do not despair,
For God will answer you, sometime, somewhere.

Unanswered yet? But you are not unheeded;
The promises of God forever stand;
To Him our days and years alike are equal.
"Have faith in God!" It is your Lord's command.
Hold on to Jacob's angel, and your prayer
Shall bring a blessing down, sometime, somewhere.

OPHELIA G. BROWNING

Being confident of this very thing,
that He which hath begun a good work in you
will perform it until the day of Jesus Christ.
P H I L I P P I A N S   1 : 6

What I do thou knowest not now;
but thou shalt know hereafter.
J O H N   1 3 : 7

Unanswered yet? Nay do not say unanswered;
Perhaps your part is not yet wholly done.
The work began when first your prayer was uttered,
And God will finish what He has begun.
Keep incense burning at the shrine of prayer,
And glory shall descend, sometime, somewhere.

Unanswered yet? Faith cannot be unanswered;
Her feet are firmly planted on the Rock,
Amid the wildest storms she stands undaunted,
Nor quails before the loudest thunder shock.
She knows Omnipotence has heard her prayer,
And cries, "It shall be done, sometime, somewhere."

O P H E L I A   G .   B R O W N I N G

*P*rayer inbreathed by the Spirit of God is part
of His working in bringing about the event,
and what He begins He is able to and will finish.
Prayer needs to be persevered in because it is so completely a part of God's plan in bringing the blessing.

Ye also helping together by prayer for us.
2   C O R I N T H I A N S   1 : 1 1

A station in the China Inland Mission was peculiarly blessed of God. Inquirers were more numerous and more easily turned from dumb idols to serve the living God than at other stations. The difference was a theme of conversation and wonder. In England J. Hudson Taylor was warmly greeted at a certain place by a stranger who showed great interest in his mission work. He was so particular and intelligent in his questions concerning one missionary and the locality in which he labored, seemed so well acquainted with his helpers, inquirers, and the difficulties of that particular station, that Mr. Taylor's curiosity was aroused to find out the reason of this intimate knowledge. He now learned that this stranger and the successful missionary had covenanted together as co-workers. The missionary kept his home brother informed of all the phases of his labor. He gave him the names of inquirers, stations, hopeful characters and difficulties, and all these the home worker was wont to spread out before God in prevailing prayer.

A. T. PIERSON

And it shall come to pass, that before they call, I will
answer: and while they are yet speaking I will hear.
I S A I A H   6 5 : 2 4

A young man in New York was deeply concerned for the salvation of his father in
Massachusetts. He left the Fulton Street prayer-meeting and took passage on a Long Island Sound steamer.
He spent nearly all the night in his stateroom wrestling
in prayer for his father. On reaching home the next
evening he took down the Bible and said, "Father, let
us read a chapter in the Bible and pray!" "Certainly,"
said the father, "you read." After reading, his father led
off in prayer, pouring forth the most earnest petitions.
"Father," said the son, as they rose from their knees,
"how long is it since God gave you a heart to pray?" "I
began last night. I was awakened in the night, and cried
to God for mercy, and He has had mercy upon me."

How many souls there are which may be reached
and saved through prayer. We can touch men by way
of the throne of God when we cannot touch them in
any other way. Are you praying for some unsaved rel-
ative or friend?

Thy prayers are come up for a memorial before God.

ACTS 10:4

*I*t would seem almost as if supplications of years had accumulated before the Throne, and at last the answer broke in blessings on the head of Cornelius, even as the accumulated evaporation of months at last bursts in floods of rain upon the dry ground. So God is represented as treasuring the prayers of His saints in vials; they are described as sweet odors. They are placed like fragrant flowers in the chambers of the King, and kept in sweet remembrance before Him. And later they are represented as poured out upon the earth; and lo, there are voices and thunderings and great providential movements fulfilling God's purposes for His kingdom. We are called "the Lord's remembrancers," and are commanded to give Him no rest, day nor night, but crowd the heavens with our petitions and in due time the answer will come with its accumulated blessings.

A. B. SIMPSON

What an encouragement the text for today should be in our prayer-life! The more prayer, the broader and deeper the river of blessing that shall flow forth as the result.

And it came to pass, that when I was come again to Jerusalem, even while I prayed in the temple, I was in a trance. And saw Him saying unto me, make haste, and get thee quickly out of Jerusalem. . . . And He said unto me, Depart; for I will send thee far hence unto the Gentiles.

ACTS 22:17, 18, 21

With everything thus begun, continued and ended in prayer, marking every emergency, animating every act of wider obedience (in the early Church) is it any wonder that when the flames of missionary zeal and success sank away, it was because the fires of prayer had died low on the altars of devotion? Is there any other reason than this for the reiterated plea in the Epistles of Paul, that the churches he had founded would labor together with him in prayer for the prosperity of the gospel with them, and with him in all the world? No. The first two things in the early Church were prayer and missions, and the deepest alliance in the early Church was between missions and prayer.

ROBERT E. SPEER

I will pour water on him that is thirsty, and floods upon the dry ground: I will pour My spirit upon thy seed, and My blessing upon thine offspring.

ISAIAH 44:3

We must keep on praying and waiting upon the Lord, until the sound of a mighty rain is heard. There is no reason why we should not ask for large things. And without doubt we shall get large things if we ask in faith, and have the courage to wait with patient perseverance upon Him, meantime doing those things which lie within our power to do. We cannot create the wind or set it in motion, but we can set our sails to catch it when it comes; we cannot make the electricity, but we can stretch the wire along upon which it is to run and do its work; we cannot in a word, control the Spirit, but we can so place ourselves before the Lord, and so do the things He has bidden us do that we will come under the influence and power of His mighty breath.

THE INDEPENDENT

The promise of God's outpouring of blessing inspires us to pray for its coming. God will be ready to give great things quite as soon as we are to receive them.

I will bless the Lord at all times:
His praise shall continually be in my mouth.

P S A L M   3 4 : 1

*A*t all times," in every situation, under every circumstance, before, in and after trials, in bright days of glee, and dark nights of fear. He would never have done praising, because never satisfied that he had done enough; always feeling that he fell short of the Lord's deservings. Happy is he whose fingers are wedded to his harp. He who praises God for mercies shall never want a mercy for which to praise. To bless the Lord is never unreasonable.

Our thankfulness is not to be a dumb thing; it should be one of the daughters of music.

C . H . S P U R G E O N

From the first chapter of the Epistle to the Romans we learn that thanklessness was one of the first steps the race took in departing from God (Romans 1:21). When they ceased to be thankful they soon drifted far away from God, until they sank into the most abominable heathenism. We need to be very watchful lest we become thankless and go from thanklessness to prayerlessness.

And when she came to Solomon, she communed with him of all that was in her heart. And Solomon told her all her questions: and there was nothing hid from Solomon which he told her not.

2 C H R O N I C L E S 9 : 1 , 2

I came and communed with that mighty King,
And told Him all my heart; I cannot say
In mortal ear what communings were they.
But wouldst thou then know, go too,
    and meekly bring
All that is in thy heart, and thou shalt hear,
His voice of love and power,
His answers sweet and clear.

Oh, happy end of every weary quest!
He told me all I needed, graciously—
Enough for guidance, and for victory
O'er doubts and fears, enough for quiet rest;
And when some veiled response I could not read,
It was not hid from Him—
his was enough indeed.

F. R. HAVERGAL

Tell Him all that is in thy heart. He knoweth how to solve thy hard questions, and make all thy perplexities clear. Trust Him to unravel thy mysteries, and then give Him time to make known to thee what is not hid from Him.

And at midnight Paul and Silas prayed,
and sang praises unto God.

ACTS   16:25

*L*et all lovers of souls, and all workers in the service of the gospel, take courage. Time spent in
prayer will yield more than that given to work. Prayer
alone gives work its worth and its success. Prayer
opens the way for God Himself to do His work in us
and through us. Let our chief work, as God's messen-
gers, be intercession; in it we secure the presence and
power of God to go with us.

ANDREW MURRAY

"Time spent in prayer will yield more than that given
to work." How little do we show that we believe it,
indeed practically we do not believe it. When work
crowds us we hurry through prayer, and crowd it into
a narrower corner. Then we work with less wisdom,
less power, less success. Oh, that we might learn to put
the first things first. When work precedes prayer, or is
without prayer it becomes an effort of the flesh. When
prayer comes first, then the work is the mighty operation of the Holy Spirit and must succeed.

Then said the priest, Let us draw near hither unto God. And Saul asked counsel of God, Shall I go down after the Philistines? wilt Thou deliver them into the hand of Israel? But He answered him not that day.

1   S A M U E L   1 4 : 3 6 ,   3 7

*P*rayer is not human whim, but holy desire offered up for things according to the will of God. It is not a man imposing his test on God, but God proposing the line along which, in His promises, we may prove Him. Prayer sees Him always on the throne to grant or to deny, answering equally in either case. It never discrowns the God it addresses. Let no man think the less of true prayer for that rashness of interpretation which, under color of honoring prayer, is really dishonorable to God.

D . W . F A U N C E

Never have men made a greater mistake than when their praying has been the imposing of a test upon God, when in their praying they wanted God to bend to their self-will, when before their praying they have made up their minds to pursue a certain course anyway. Prayer must indeed be more than a human whim.

Praying always.

E P H E S I A N S   6 : 1 8

Pray, always pray! the Holy Spirit pleads
Within thee all thy daily, hourly needs.
Pray, always pray! Beneath sin's heaviest load
Prayer sees the blood from Jesus' side that flowed.
Pray, always pray! Though weary, faint and alone!
Prayer nestles by the Father's sheltering throne.
Pray, always pray! Amid the world's turmoil
Prayer keeps the heart at rest, and nerves for toil.
Pray, always pray! If joys the pathway throng
Prayer strikes the harp and sings the angels' song.
Pray, always pray! If loved ones pass the rail,
Prayer drinks with them of springs that cannot fail.
All earthly things with earth shall pass away;
Prayer grasps eternity; pray, always pray.

B I S H O P   E. H. B I C K E R S T E T H

*P*rayer fits into every phase of our earthly experience, and therefore we may always pray. Your present need, difficulty, trouble may be taken to God in prayer. There is nothing in our life in which our Heavenly Father is not interested. "Ask and ye shall receive."

O Thou that hearest prayer,
unto Thee shall all flesh come.

PSALM 65 : 2

*T*his shall encourage men of all nations to become suppliants to the one and only God, who proves His Deity by answering those who seek His face. Flesh they are, and therefore weak; frail and sinful, they need to pray; and Thou art such a God as they need, for Thou art touched with compassion, and dost condescend to hear the cries of poor flesh and blood. Many come to Thee now in humble faith, and are filled with good, but more shall be drawn to Thee by the attractiveness of Thy love, and at length the whole earth shall bow at Thy feet. To come to God is the life of true religion; we come weeping in conversion, hoping in supplication, rejoicing in praise, and delighting in service.

C. H. SPURGEON

Man prays because he finds his true counterpart in God. He is a spiritual being and God is a spirit, therefore he may pray. When made a new creature in the image of Him who created him, it becomes natural for man to pray.

*And Jacob said, O God of my father Abraham,
and God of my father Isaac, the Lord which saidst
unto me, Return unto thy country, and to thy kindred, and I will deal well with thee. I am not worthy
of the least of all the mercies, and of all the truth,
which Thou hast shewed unto Thy servant; for with
my staff I passed over this Jordan; and now I am
become two bands. Deliver me, I pray Thee, from the
hand of my brother, from the hand of Esau.*

G E N E S I S   3 2 : 9 - 1 1

*I*t does not seem that there could be a finer
model for a special prayer than this—the most
ancient of all. He first claims his interest in the
covenant with Abraham and Isaac, just as we might,
and ought to, set forth our interest in the mercies
covenanted to us in Christ; then he urges the covenant
of personal mercies and promises: then he confesses
his utter unworthiness of the blessings that have been
showered upon him, yet venturing, notwithstanding to
hope for deliverance from the danger that lay before
him.

J O H N   K I T T O

The foundations on which we build the superstructure
of prayer are broad and firm.

We know not what we should pray for as we ought.

ROMANS 8:26

*W*hen a man breaks down and cannot pray, and there is a fire burning in his heart, and a burden resting upon him, there is something drawing him to God. "I know not what to pray"—oh blessed ignorance! We are not ignorant enough. Abraham went out not knowing whither he went; in that was an element of ignorance and also an element of faith. Jesus said to His disciples when they came with their prayer for the throne, "Ye know not what ye ask." Paul says, "No man knoweth the things of God but the Spirit of God." You say, "If I am not to pray the old prayers I learned from my mother, or from my professor in college, or from my experience yesterday and the day before, what am I to pray?" I answer, pray new prayers, rise higher into the riches of God.

ANDREW MURRAY

NEW PRAYERS! Nothing do we need so much as to keep out of old ruts in prayer. How much of the language of prayer is stereotyped. Prayer will be new when Spirit-taught.

*I have heard their cry by reason of their taskmasters;
for I know their sorrows; and I am come
down to deliver them.*

E X O D U S   3 : 7 ,   8

*P*rayer has all along preceded God's redemption movements on behalf of men. The cry in Egypt was not simply a cry of woe because of the bitterness of the bondage; it was a cry of prayer to God for deliverance. The return of the Jews from Babylonian captivity was preceded by the prayers of such men as Daniel, Nehemiah and Ezra. Simeon and Anna represented the company of those who were looking to God for the fulfillment of the promises of the coming of the Messiah. The present dispensation was inaugurated by the ten days' prayer meeting of one hundred and twenty disciples. The return of the Jews to their own land again is to be accompanied by a new spirit of prayer and supplication. And will not the second coming of Christ have as its precursor a widespread revival of the spirit of prayer among God's people? When the church earnestly prays for the coming of Christ the event will not be far off.

CHARLES A COOK

Casting all your care upon Him;
for He careth for you.

1 P E T E R   5 : 7

*T*here are two or three preliminaries before
this committal of care is possible. We must
have cast our sins before we can cast our cares; in
other words, we must be children in the Father's home.
Then also we must be living in God's plan, sure that
we are where He would have us be, camped under His
brooding pillar-cloud. And, in addition, we must have
yielded up our lives to Him, for Him to have His way
in them. Nor must we neglect to feed our faith with
promise. Without her natural food she pines. But when
these conditions are fulfilled, it is not difficult to

> Kneel, and cast our load,
> E'en while we pray, upon our God.
> Then rise with lightened cheer.

The cup may still have to be drunk, the discipline
borne, the work done; but the weary ache of care will
have yielded to the anodyne of a child's trust in One
who cannot fail.

F. B. M E Y E R

Without Me ye can do nothing.
J O H N   1 5 : 5

*H*ow do you ever get through your work,"
one asked of a gentleman, the proprietor
of vast enterprises involving millions and employing
hundreds. "You are a Christian, and can understand
me," was the reply. "I never could get through it all
without Christ. I regard myself simply as managing
this business for Him as the true proprietor. I take to
Him, therefore, all the embarrassments and perplexities, and He carries the burdens and receives the
returns, while I am His steward and servant."

WAYLAND HOYT

The Christian's life is a partnership with Jesus, and He
is the chief partner. It is our privilege not only to consult Him in all the affairs of our life, but to draw on
His infinite resources in the assurance that He will supply all our need. Prayer is having a conference with the
chief partner, and should ever be characterized by the
greatest freedom and fullest confidence. There must be
something wrong when a Christian cannot talk to God
about his daily business.

I have set watchmen on thy walls
which shall never hold their peace day nor
night: ye that are the Lord's remembrances, keep
not silence and give Him no rest.

ISAIAH 62:6

*R*obert Murray McCheyne drew up the following to govern him in his prayer-life: "I am persuaded that I ought never to do anything without prayer, and, if possible, special secret prayer. . . . I ought to pray far more for my own church, for the leading ministers by name, and for my own clear guidance in the right way, that I may not be led aside, or driven aside from following Christ. . . . . I should pray much more in peaceful days, that I may be guided rightly when days of trial come. I ought to spend the best hours of the day in communion with God. It is my noblest and most fruitful employment, and is not to be thrust into any corner."

Have we come to realize the truth of that last sentence for ourselves? If we make as much of prayer, as some of these men of God did, we shall undoubtedly find it our most fruitful employment. Let us set apart a time for special prayer and intercession today.

My soul thirsteth for God,
for the living God.

P S A L M   4 2 : 2

*T*hey are happy in their very yearnings who are
conscious of the true direction of these, and
can say it is God for whom they are athirst. All unrest
of longing, all fever of thirst, all outgoings of desire, are
feelers put out blindly and are only stilled when they
clasp Him. The correspondence between man's needs
and their true object is involved in that name "the living God"; for a heart can rest only in one all-sufficient
Person, and must have a heart to throb against. Neither
obstructions nor dead things can still its cravings. That
which does must be living. But no finite being can still
them; and after all sweetnesses of human loves and
helps of human strengths, the soul's thirst remains
unslaked, and the Person who is enough must be the
living God.

A L E X A N D E R   M A C L A R E N

In prayer the soul finds its way to this living, all-satis-
fying fountain, and receives of the infinite fullness in
God, and goes on its way refreshed, filled with new
strength, and encouraged to come again and again to
receive ever fresh supplies.

He shall baptize you with the
Holy Ghost, and with fire.
M A T T H E W   3 : 1 1

W hen a lecturer on electricity wants to show an example of a human body surcharged with his fire, he places a person on a stool with glass legs. The glass serves to isolate him from the earth, because it will not conduct the fire—the electric fluid: were it not for this, however much might be poured into his frame, it would be carried away by the earth, but when thus isolated from it, he retains all that enters him. . . . If then, thou wouldst have thy soul surcharged with the fire of God, so that those who come nigh to thee shall feel some mysterious influence proceeding out from thee, thou must draw nigh to the source of that fire, to the throne of God and of the Lamb, and shut thyself out from the world—that cold world, which so swiftly steals our fire away. Enter into thy closet, and shut thy door, and there, isolated, "before the throne" await the baptism; then the fire shall fill thee, and thou shalt labor, not in thine own strength, but "with demonstration of the Spirit, and with power."

W I L L I A M   A R T H U R

*In everything by prayer and supplication
with thanksgiving, let your requests
be made known unto God.*

PHILIPPIANS 4 : 6

*I*n the hour alone let us speak quite out, into the Lord's ears, the very thing, the very need, the very temptation, yes, and the very discovery of the grace that is for us in Christ, which then and there is present to the soul. Let us rescue our friends, not formally, as if the mere naming of them had an efficacy in it, but as realizing the individuals before the Lord and so presenting them to Him. Let us be freely explicit about them, about anything. Let us take our blessed Master into confidence. He invites it, He loves it.

H. C. G. MOULE

How a child pours out its heart to its mother, telling all its grief and woe. And then how tenderly the mother comforts the distressed heart. So will He comfort us. Isaiah 66:13.

Oft I tell Him I am weary, and I fain would be at rest;
That I'm daily, hourly, longing to repose upon His breast;
And He answers me so kindly, in the tenderest tones of love,
I am coming soon to take thee to my happy home above.

But unto Thee, O Lord, have I cried, And in the morning shall my prayer come before Thee.

P S A L M 8 8 : 1 3 , R . V .

*V*ery earnestly would I advise the dedication to secret prayer of a strictly regular time; a punctual beginning, and, especially in the morning, a measured and liberal allotment. I certainly do not mean a mere mechanical regularity, as if we watched the clock for the moment when to close. But I do mean a time at least as punctual and at least as free from hurry as that which we habitually give to our meals; and this, I repeat, especially in the morning. If I plead less earnestly for a large allowance of time at night I do it with hesitation and reserve, and only because a conscientious Christian, who is doing the will of God through the day, is likely to be physically tired at night in a way in which he will not be, certainly in his youth, in the morning.

H . C . G . M O U L E

One of the greatest hindrances to prayer is the hurry of life, the pressure and rush of business. In the interests of our soul we must guard ourselves at this point, and take time to pray.

*Today thy servant knoweth that I have found grace
in thy sight, my lord, O King, in that the king
hath fulfilled the request of his servant.*

2   S A M U E L   1 4 : 2 2

*P*ersonal acceptance comes first. We must be "accepted in the Beloved" before we can look to be answered through the Beloved. Is there a doubt about this, and a sigh over the words? There need not be; for now, at this moment, the old promise stands with its unchangeable welcome to the weary: "Him that cometh to me I will in no wise cast out." Then if you come, now, at this moment, on the strength of His word, you cannot be rejected; and if not rejected, there is nothing but one blessed alternative—"accepted."

F. R. HAVERGAL

What liberty in prayer is inspired by the assurance of our personal acceptance in the Beloved. Let us lay hold of our standing in Christ by faith, and we shall pray better and with more joy and blessing. The assurance that we are ourselves accepted will inspire the confidence that our prayers are also accepted. If we are not accepted, how can our prayers be?

He that dwelleth in the secret place of the Most High,
shall abide under the shadow of the Almighty.

P S A L M   9 1 : 1

*T*here is no short cut to the life of faith, which is the all-vital condition of a holy and victorious life. We must have periods of lonely meditation and fellowship with God. That our souls should have their mountains of fellowship, their valleys of quiet rest beneath the shadow of a great rock, their nights beneath the stars, when darkness has veiled the material and silenced the stir of human life, and has opened the view of the infinite and eternal, is as indispensable as that our bodies should have food. Thus alone can the sense of God's presence become the fixed possession of the soul, enabling it to say repeatedly, with the psalmist, "Thou art near, O God."

F. B. MEYER

Conscious nearness to God, entering into the inner sanctuary where His glory shineth, is both the inestimable privilege and the indispensable essential of true prayer. To pray without a consciousness of God, without fellowship with Him is to make prayer empty and powerless.

Evening, and morning, and at noon, will I pray,
and cry aloud: and He shall hear my voice.

P S A L M   5 5 : 1 7

Pray when the morning breaketh,
Pray when the noon shines bright,
Pray in the evening gloaming,
Pray thro' the long dark night.
Pray in the secret closet,
Pray with beloved of home,
Pray in the house of worship,
Pray wheresoe'er you roam.
Pray for beloved kindred,
Pray for your friends so dear,
Pray for your chance associates,
Pray for the foes you fear.
Pray for the church of Jesus,
Pray for the pastor true,
Pray for her chosen rulers,
Pray for the members too.
Pray with a heart believing,
Pray with a fervent mind,
Pray with a lowly spirit,
Pray with a will resigned.

C H A R L E S   M .   F I L L M O R E

The need and the field for prayer are boundless.
Oh, for grace to more fully occupy the field to
the glory of God.

And Samuel cried unto the Lord for Israel; and the Lord heard him. . . . The Lord thundered with a great thunder on that day upon the Philistines and discomfited them. . . . And the men of Israel went out of Mizpah, and pursued the Philistines, and smote them, until they came under Beth-car.

1   S A M U E L   7 : 9 - 1 1

*H*ere is a deeply practical lesson for our prayer-life. Samuel's prayer for the people was preceded by fasting and confession of sin, and devout turning unto the Lord on their part; see verses 3, 4. It was preceded by the offering of a whole burnt-offering unto the Lord, and the burnt-offering symbolized completeness of consecration unto God. When we have wholly turned away from sin, and wholly surrendered ourselves to God, we can look up to God in prayer for deliverance from the Philistines that beset us. God will never forsake a people yielded up to Him, but will interpose mightily on their behalf.

The people followed up the divine interposition by their own earnest action. We are to work in the line of our prayers.

CHARLES A. COOK

Let the words of my mouth, and the meditation
of my heart, be acceptable in Thy sight, O Lord,
my strength, and my redeemer.

P S A L M   1 9 : 1 4

✻

*I*t must be confessed that some good men, afraid
of forms, allow to themselves a kind of rambling in prayer which they could never employ elsewhere. Word suggests word, and the prayer is without
form and void. An address to man, as inconsequential,
as incoherent would be absurd. Such a prayer written
out would amaze the man who offers it. A letter to a
friend would have at least some general order. . . . Shall
we permit ourselves, in this miscellaneous address to
God, rambling repetitions, sentences without connection, words used because we have heard them
employed repeatedly in family or public prayer, with
pauses in which one stops to think what next is to be
said and fills up the gap by using some one of the
many names of God—are these the prayers that can
claim answers?

D . W . F A U N C E

Incoherence in prayer utterance indicates thoughtless-
ness and irreverence, and should be earnestly guarded
against.

And it came to pass on the morrow, that Moses said unto the people, ye have sinned a great sin: and now I will go up unto the Lord; peradventure I shall make an atonement for your sin.

E X O D U S   3 2 : 3 0

eing for the people to Godward" became more and more characteristic of the life of Moses. Whenever the people cried unto him, he prayed unto the Lord. When the spirit of revolt spread through the camp he fell upon his face. When it seemed likely that the whole nation must perish for their sin, he stood in the breach and besought the Lord, and turned away the destruction that hung over them like a lurid cloud. Twice for forty days their interests detained him in the holy mount. And in long years after, he is classed with Samuel as one who had stood before God for his people.

F. B. MEYER

Reader—art thou "for the people to Godward"? It is a great ministry involving great responsibilities, but is it not for this ministry that we are taught how to pray? Let us not shrink from the task but gratefully take it up for the world's sake.

*And continueth in supplications
and prayers night and day.*
1   T I M O T H Y   5 : 5

*Ye that are the Lord's remembrancers,
keep not silence, and give Him no rest till He
make Jerusalem a praise in the earth.*
I S A I A H   6 2 : 6 ,   7

*G*od seeks intercessors. He will not, He cannot, take the work out of His Church. And so He comes, calling and pleading in many ways. Now by a man whom He raises up to live a life of faith in His service, and to prove how actually and abundantly He answers prayer; then by the story of a church which makes prayer for souls its starting-point and bears testimony to God's faithfulness.

In these and many other ways God is showing us what intercession can do, and beseeching us to waken up and train His great host to be, every one, a people of intercessors.

A N D R E W   M U R R A Y

The world's need is an army of intercessors who will pray for the spread of the gospel to the uttermost ends of the earth.

*Then they cried unto the Lord in their trouble, and
He delivered them out of their distresses.*

P S A L M 1 0 7 : 6

*S*cenes of deep distress await us all. Of one
thing we may be assured, that if the trials are
not removed, yet our supplications will not be in vain;
we shall be enabled to bear them. And we may expect,
and expect with confidence, that a more than Angelic
Comforter, even the Spirit of truth, will shed His healing influence over our souls, and preserve us from
sinking under the severest trials.

B I S H O P P O R T E U S

Supplications which are forced out of us by stern necessity are none the less acceptable with God; but indeed,
they have all the more prevalence since they are evidently
sincere and make a powerful appeal to the divine pity.

C . H . S P U R G E O N

There hath no temptation taken you, but such
as is common to man; but God is faithful, who will not
suffer you to be tempted above that ye are able; but
will with the temptation also make a way to escape,
that ye may be able to bear it. 1 Corinthians 10:13.

What encouragement to prayer is this!

I waited patiently for the Lord; and
He inclined unto me, and heard my cry.
P S A L M   4 0 : 1

Neither Jesus the head, nor any of the members of His body, shall ever wait upon the Lord in vain. Mark the figure of inclining, as though the suppliant cried out of the lowest depression, and condescending love stooped to hear his feeble moans. What a marvel is it that our Lord Jesus should have to cry as we do, and wait as we do, and should receive the Father's help after the same process of faith and pleading as must be gone through by ourselves! The Saviour's prayers among the midnight mountains and in Gethsemane expounded this verse. The son of David was brought low, but He rose to victory; and here He teaches us how to conduct our conflicts so as to succeed after the same glorious pattern of triumph. Let us arm ourselves with the same mind; and panoplied in patience, armed with prayer, and girt with faith, let us maintain the Holy War.

C. H. SPURGEON

Patience is an important lesson anywhere, but nowhere so important as in our prayer-life.

*Let Thy work appear unto Thy servants,
and Thy glory unto their children.*

PSALM   90:16

❋

*T*he objection which often hinders our praying, or praying in confidence of results—
namely, that we are entirely helpless to effect any
result—is the grand reason for praying; and when such
praying is answered, the evidence of God's working is
irresistible. It is when we are in trouble and refuge fails
us, when we are at our wits' end, that it becomes plain
that He saves us out of our distresses. Unbelief is
always ready to suggest that it is not a strange thing if
a prayer for the conversion of another is answered,
when we have been bending every energy toward the
winning of a soul; and we find it very hard to say how
far the result is traceable to God and how far to man.
But when one can do nothing but cry to God, and yet
He works mightily to save, unbelief is silenced, or
compelled to confess, this is the finger of God.

A. T. PIERSON

What we should seek in praying is some clear manifestation of God's working. We may always pray, "Let
Thy work appear unto Thy servants."

Ask ye of the Lord rain in the time of the latter rain;
so the Lord shall make bright clouds, and give them
showers of rain, to every one grass in the field.

Z E C H A R I A H   1 0 : 1

Ask of Me, and I shall give thee the
heathen for thine inheritance.

P S A L M   2 : 8

Considering the fearful consequences of it all, something like criminal negligence has marked for years the attitude of the church toward the matchless power of prayer for the world. Shall it be so longer or shall a change come over the church? It will not avail to pass resolutions and form prayer alliances. For generations great calls have been issued, leagues have been proposed, emotions have been aroused, and yet the days continue evil; the kingdom of God moves but slowly still, and prayer is an echo on men's lips rather than a passion from their hearts. But if fifty men of our generation will enter the holy place of prayer, and become, henceforth, men whose hearts God has touched with the prayer-passion, the history of His Church would be changed.

ROBERT E. SPEER

Let the word of Christ
dwell in you richly in all wisdom.

C O L O S S I A N S   3 : 1 6

*T*he inspired Scriptures form the vehicle of the Spirit in communicating to us the knowledge of the will of God. If we think of God on the one side and man on the other, the Word of God is the mode of conveyance from God to man, of His own mind and heart. It therefore becomes a channel prepared by the Spirit for the purpose, and unspeakably sacred as such. When therefore the believer uses the Word of God as the guide to determine both the spirit and the dialect of his prayer, he is inverting the process of divine revelation and using the channel of God's approach to him as the channel of his approach to God. How can such use of God's Word fail to help and strengthen spiritual life? What medium or channel of approach could so insure in the praying soul both an acceptable frame and language taught by the Spirit?

A. T. PIERSON
IN *GEORGE MÜLLER OF BRISTOL*

God's plan seems to be that men shall approach Him by the same way that He approaches them.

Lest Satan should get an advantage of us:
for we are not ignorant of his devices.

2   C O R I N T H I A N S   2 : 1 1

I t is a common temptation of Satan to make us give up the reading of the Word and prayer when our enjoyment is gone; as if it were of no use to read the Scriptures when we do not enjoy them, and as if it were of no use to pray when we have no spirit of prayer; whilst the truth is, in order to enjoy the Word, we ought to continue to read it, and the way to obtain a spirit of prayer is to continue praying; for the less we read the Word of God, the less we desire to read it, and the less we pray, the less we desire to pray.

GEORGE MÜLLER

Satan has many ways of ensnaring God's children, but when he seeks to hinder our prayer-life he attacks the very citadel of our spirituality and power. Here therefore let us most resolutely repel him, and at his every approach resort more earnestly to prayer.

Prayer itself is the very best protection to the spirit of prayer. "Watch and pray that ye enter not into temptation." Matthew 26:41.

And shall not God avenge His elect,
which cry to Him day and night, and
He is long-suffering over them?

L U K E   1 8 : 7

*B*ehold! the husbandman waiteth for the
precious fruit of the earth, being long-suf-
fering over it, till it receive the early and the latter rain!
The husbandman does indeed long for the harvest,
but knows that it must have its full time of sunshine
and rain, and has long patience. A child so often
wants to pick the half-ripe fruit; the husbandman
knows to wait till the proper time. . . . And it is the
Father, in whose hands are the times and seasons,
who alone knows the moment when the soul or the
church is ripened to that fullness of faith in which it
can really take and keep the blessing. As a father who
longs to have his only child home from school, and
yet waits patiently till the time of training is completed,
so it is with God and His children: He is the long-suffering one and answers speedily.

A N D R E W   M U R R A Y

Learn in prayer not only to wait on the Lord but also
to wait for the Lord. Isaiah 30:18.

Whoso offereth praise glorifieth me.

PSALM 50:23

*T*he love that seeks to bless us desires, as all love does, that it should be known for what it is, that it should be recognized in our glad hearts, and smiled back again from our brightened faces. God desires that we should know Him, and so have Eternal Life; He desires that knowing Him we should love Him, and loving should praise, and so glorify Him. He desires that there should be an interchange of love bestowing and love receiving, of gifts showered down, of praise ascending, of fire falling from the heavens, and sweet incense from grateful hearts, going up in fragrant clouds acceptable unto God.

ALEXANDER MACLAREN

Hast thou presented thine offering of praise today—didst thou do so yesterday? God's love is ever bestowing; is our love ever praising? As our blessings abound, so should our gratitude. Every day should be Thanksgiving Day, every season of prayer have its song of praise.

My soul, wait thou only upon God;
for my expectation is from Him.

P S A L M   6 2 : 5

*W*e expect from God because we believe in Him. Expectation is the child of prayer and faith, and is owned of the Lord as an acceptable grace. We should desire nothing but what it would be right for God to give, and then our expectation would be all from God; and concerning really good things we should not look to second causes, but to the Lord alone, and so again our expectation should be all from Him. The vain expectations of worldly men come not; they promise, but there is no performance; our expectations are on the way, and in due season will arrive to satisfy our hopes. Happy is the man who feels that all he has, all he wants, and all he expects are to be found in his God.

C. H. SPURGEON

"Expect great things from God," uttered William Carey, and inaugurated the modern missionary movement, and as we expect great things from God, pray for great things, and work for great things, great things shall be seen. Our expectations will be great as we base them on God's faithfulness.

O come, let us worship and bow down:
let us kneel before the Lord our maker.

PSALM   95:6

*T*here are different phases of prayer. There is worship, when a man just bows down to adore the great God. We do not take time to worship. We need to worship in secret, just to get ourselves face to face with the everlasting God, that He may over-shadow us and cover us and fill us with His love and His glory. It is the Holy Spirit who can work in us such a yearning that we will give up our pleasures, and even a part of our business, that we may the oftener meet our God.

ANDREW MURRAY

Prayer has to do with our needs, or the needs of oth-ers; worship has to do with God Himself. In worship the heart is occupied with Him. The more we really worship God the more truly spiritual and holy will be our praying. "Lord, fix my wandering thoughts on Thyself in sincerest worship, that for a time I may for-get all my needs and be occupied wholly with Thy glory. Help me to take more time to worship Thee."

Let the Lord do that which is good in His sight.

1 CHRONICLES 19:13

*T*hat prayer which does not succeed in moderating our wish, in changing the passionate desire into still submission, the anxious, tumultuous expectation into silent surrender, is no true prayer, and proves that we have not the spirit of true prayer. That life is most holy in which there is least of petition and desire, and most of waiting upon God; that in which petition most often passes into thanksgiving. Pray till prayer makes you forget your own wish, and leave it or merge it in God's will. The divine wisdom has given us prayer, not as a means to obtain the good things of earth, but as a means whereby we learn to do without them; not as a means whereby we escape evil but as a means whereby we become strong to meet it.

F. W. ROBERTSON

What a remarkable lesson is brought to us in our thought for today, that prayer is a means whereby we learn to do without the good things of earth. What abiding peace it will bring us if we learn this lesson well.

Draw nigh to God and He will draw nigh to you.

J A M E S   4 : 8

Truly our fellowship is with the Father,
and with His Son Jesus Christ.

1   J O H N   1 : 3

*T*he object of prayer is not to inform God; but it is to train us in habits of personal inter-course with God, of personal sonship toward Him. We are made for sonship—sonship is personal correspon-dence, personal intelligent cooperation with God. It is a gradually increasing power of familiarity with God; of intercourse with Him, of approach toward Him as person to person. Thus, prayer is made necessary for us simply in order that by this necessity for praying, for asking, we may be as it were, constrained again and again to come before God, and by asking, familiarize ourselves with Him; and as we ask, and as we receive, grow into correspondence with God our Father.

C .   G O R E

Fellowship with the Father and with His Son has a trans-forming power. By the process of prayer, the image of Christ in us grows. God is making a race of men like His Son. Prayer is one of His ways of doing the work.

Lord, hear my voice: let Thine ears be attentive
to the voice of my supplications.

P S A L M 1 3 0 : 2

*T*he great Author of Nature and of all things does nothing in vain. He instituted not this law, and if I may so express it, art of praying as a vain and insignificant thing, but endows it with a wonderful efficacy for producing the greatest and happiest consequences. He would have it to be the key by which all the treasures of heaven should be opened. He has constructed it as a powerful machine, by which we may with ease and pleasant labor remove from us the most dire and unhappy machinations of our enemy, and may with equal ease draw to ourselves what is most propitious and advantageous. Heaven and earth and all the elements obey and minister to the hands which are often lifted up to heaven in earnest prayer.

R. LEIGHTON

Thy prayers will not be in vain. The Lord thy God will hear thee, for in praying thou art in line with His own way of working. Be encouraged to continue to pray because God has instituted the law of prayer. In harmony with the law there is blessing.

*And the publican, standing afar off, would not lift
up so much as his eyes unto heaven, but smote upon
his breast, saying, God be merciful to me a sinner.*

*T*he question is often asked, "Shall we get unconverted people to pray?" What do you mean by
unconverted people? If a man is sorry for his sin, and
wishes to forsake it and find mercy, and is willing to
humble himself before God and ask for pardon, he is
taking the very steps by which a man turns around, or
is "converted." To tell a man he must not pray under
such circumstances, is to tell him that he must not be
converted until he is converted; that he must not turn
until he is turned around. To get him to pray is just the
thing to do. "For whosoever shall call upon the name of
the Lord shall be saved." Romans 10:13

R. A. TORREY

Prayer is the most natural thing for a penitent soul.
Hast thou sinned? Make the fifty-first Psalm thy prayer.
The Prodigal's resolve was "I will arise and go to my
father." The returning of the sinner to God is itself a
prayer.

Casting all your care upon Him;
for He careth for you.

1   P E T E R   5 : 7

*T*reat cares as you treat sins. Hand them over to Jesus one by one as they occur. Commit them to Him. Roll them upon Him. Make them His. By an act of faith look to Him, saying, "This Lord, and this, and this, I cannot bear. Thou hast taken my sins; take my cares: I lay them upon Thee, and trust Thee to do for me all, and more than all, I need. I will trust and not be afraid." As George Herbert says so quaintly in his sonnet, "Put care into Christ's bag." There is no surer path to rest than to pass on to Jesus all the anxieties of life, believing that He takes what we give at the moment of our giving it, that it instantly becomes a matter of honor with Him to do His best for us; and surely it is a sacrilege to take back any gift which we have put into His hands.

F. B. MEYER

What a clog to all activity care is. How earnestly therefore should we seek at the beginning of every day to free ourselves from its hindering presence. Be watchful not to allow care to hinder thee in serving Christ today.

*These all continued with one accord
in prayer and supplication.*

A C T S 1 : 1 4

*C*hristians must be "of one accord" if they are to prevail with God. It is with their prayers as with music—discords destroy each other by their crashing and colliding; only the harmonies sustain and bear each other upward and onward. Guided by their own will alone, a score of Christians might all be praying at cross-purposes, one desiring this thing, and one the opposite, and each thereby nullifying the petition of the other. How shall they come to agreement? By the worldly method of getting the sense of the majority? Nay; the unity of the Spirit is the only unity that can put us in accord with heaven. Human agreements, however unanimous, are good for nothing in prayer, unless they have taken their key from God.

A. J. GORDON

It is the symphony of prayer—the symphony that comes from two or more hearts being attuned by the one spirit—that makes their praying powerful. Have I been spiritually tuned with others in prayer?

I will give thanks and sing praises unto Thy name.

2 S A M U E L 2 2 : 5 0

*And while I was speaking, and praying, and confess-
ing my sin, and the sin of my people Israel, and presenting my supplication before the Lord my God.*

D A N I E L   9 : 2 0

The very essence and speciality of secret prayer,
so it seems to me, is that it should express
most freely, whatever else it deals with, the movements
of the individual spirit, confessing inmost personal sins,
giving praise for personally received mercies, both of
providence and grace; worshipping in view of personal
insights into the Lord's great glory, supplicating regarding the deepest needs, and the simplest needs, of the
individual man, and interceding for individuals in the
freest detail and name by name. All this brings with it
the question how best to combine and adjust it all in
some such reverent order as that in our unwatched
secrecy there shall be no more idle waste of thought and
word.

H . C . G . M O U L E

Prayer undoubtedly does express "the movements of
the individual spirit." The purer the inner life, the better the praying.

*He that dwelleth in the secret place of the Most High
shall abide under the shadow of the Almighty.*

PSALM 91:1

*He went up into a mountain apart to pray: and
when the evening was come, He was there alone.*

MATTHEW 14:23

*W*hat are we to think of then as the special
difficulties of secret prayer?

I would say first, the peculiar temptation to laxity
and indolence in the practice, just because it is secret.
In the case of public prayer and social prayer, the fact
of association brings of course aid in this direction. We
are constrained by it to keep time with others, at least
to some degree, and to behave ourselves as men under
the eyes of others. But we may shorten our time of
secret prayer, we may thrust it into a corner, we may
lie late in the morning or sit up comfortably late at
night, and we are seen by no eye that we can see, and
we have no congregation to be offended by our
absence, lateness or carelessness. . . . I am sure my
reader knows, or has known, the reality of at least
some such temptations.

H. C. G. MOULE

He that hath clean hands, and a pure heart . . . He shall receive the blessing from the Lord.
PSALM   24:4,   5

When thou dost talk with God—by prayer, I mean—
Lift up pure hands; lay down all lust's desires;
Fix thoughts on heaven; present a conscience clear:
Since holy blame to mercy's throne aspires,
Confess fault's gift, crave pardon for thy sin,
Tread holy paths, call grace to guide therein.

Even as Elias, mounting to the sky,
Did cast his mantle to the earth behind,
So, when the heart presents the prayer on high,
Exclude the world from traffic with the mind:
Lips near to God, and ranging heart within,
Is but vain babbling and converts to sin.
ROBERT SOUTHWELL

Not only does God want the petition brought with clean hands, but He wants the vessel into which He pours the blessing which He bestows to be clean. 2 Timothy 2:20, 21.

Give us this day our daily bread.
M ATTHEW   6 : 1 1

*T*o wish and pray for the advantages of life is not forbidden. Our Saviour hath so far countenanced it, as to command us to pray that God would give us our daily bread; that is, as His words have already been understood, that He would bestow what is necessary for the sustenance and comfort of life. Yet the very sound of the words retrenches every superfluous and extravagant wish. Not for riches and honors, for great advancement or long life, or for numerous and flourishing families, has He given us any encouragement to pray. Foreign are such things to the real improvement, foreign very often to the true happiness of man. Foolishly they may be wished for when the wish accomplished would prove our ruin. . . . But this we may lawfully pray, that, as far as God seems meet, He would make our state comfortable, and our days easy and tranquil, and that He would save us from falling into any severe and extreme distress.

HUGH BLAIR

*I will cry unto God most high; unto God
that performeth all things for me.*

P S A L M   5 7 : 2

H e has cogent reasons for praying, for he sees God performing. The believer waits and God works. The Lord has undertaken for us, and He will not draw back; He will go through with His covenant engagements. Our translators have very properly inserted the words, "all things," for there is a blank in the Hebrew, as if it were a *carte blanche*, and you might write therein that the Lord would finish anything and everything which He has begun. Whatsoever the Lord takes in hand He will accomplish; hence past mercies are guarantees for the future, and admirable reasons for continuing to cry unto Him.

C .   H .   S P U R G E O N

When God is working most, when the church is quickened, and souls are being saved in large numbers, then let not prayer cease, for it has been often seen that great revivals, which began in prayer, began to decline when God's people left off praying. Because God performs let us pray.

Pray without ceasing.

1 T H E S S A L O N I A N S 5 : 1 7

The Christian is enjoined to pray without ceasing, not that he can always be engaged in the positive act, but he ought to have what I call a holy aptitude for prayer. The bird is not always on the wing, but he is ready to fly in an instant; so the believer is not always on the wing of prayer, but he has such a gracious aptitude for this exercise that he is prepared in an instant, when in danger or need, to fly for refuge to his God.

ROWLAND HILL

Prayer may become a habit as natural and as constant almost as breathing. We may accustom ourselves to be constantly breathing out prayer and praise to our Father in heaven. We can have many little talks with Jesus along the way, and when we do, the more distinct time of prayer will be all the more a time of sweetest fellowship with Him, and of richest blessing from Him. Our God is never far away; therefore our fellowship with Him should be constant, full and free. There should never be a moment when we could not pray. "Men ought always to pray and not to faint."

Abraham stood yet before the Lord.
GENESIS 18:22

he story takes but a few moments to read; but the scenes may have lasted for the space of hours. We cannot climb the more elevated pinnacles of prayer in a hasty rush. They demand patience, toil, prolonged endeavor, ere the lower slopes can be left, and the brooding cloud-line passed, and the aspiring soul can reach that cleft in the mountain-side, where Moses stood beneath the shadow of God's hand. Of course, our God is ever on the alert to hear and answer those prayers which, like minute-guns, we fire through the livelong day; but we cannot maintain this posture of ejaculatory prayer unless we cultivate the prolonged occasion. How much we miss because we do not wait before God. . . . If only we had remained longer at the palace door, we might have seen the King come out with a benediction in His face and a largess in His hands.

F. B. MEYER

Suppose we resolve today that henceforth we will remain "longer at the palace door," and so receive the larger blessing which the King has for us.

*I have set watchmen on thy walls which shall
never hold their peace day nor night: ye that are the
Lord's remembrancers, keep not silence,
and give Him no rest.*

*P*resident Edwards wrote of David Brainerd: "Though he was of a very sociable temper, and loved the company of saints, and delighted very much in religious conversation, and in social worship, yet his warmest affections, and their greatest effects on his animal nature, and his sweetest joys, were in his closet devotions and solitary transactions between God and his own soul; as is very observable through his whole course, from his conversion to his death. He delighted greatly in secret retirements, and loved to get quite away from all the world to converse with God alone in secret duties."

God wants a larger number of such men to be His watchmen. Are you willing to fill the office by devoting much time to prayer? More than anything else the church needs men and women in her midst who will say of every need, "Let us take this to God in prayer."

And He lifted up His hands and blessed them.
L U K E   2 4 : 5 0

*O*ne of Wellington's officers, when commanded to go on some perilous duty, lingered a moment as if afraid, and then said, "Let me have one clasp of your all-conquering hand before I go; and then I can do it." Seek the clasp of Christ's hand before every bit of work, every hard task, every battle, every good deed. Bend your head in the dewy freshness of every morning, ere you go forth to meet the day's duties and perils, and wait for the benediction of Christ, as He lays His hands upon you. They are hands of blessing. Their touch will inspire you for courage and strength and all beautiful and noble living.

J. R. MILLER

Before Moses went to his life work he stood face to face with the Lord his God, at the burning bush; before Joshua entered upon his campaign in Canaan he met the captain of the Lord's hosts near Jericho. Success will be certain, victory will be easy, if our first interview each day is with our Great Captain. What a loss must be ours if we neglect so great a privilege.

Fear thou not; for I am with thee: be not dismayed;
for I am thy God: I will strengthen thee;
yea, I will help thee; yea, I will uphold thee with
the right hand of my righteousness.

ISAIAH 41:10

*I*f we have any trial which seems intolerable, pray—pray that it be relieved or changed. . . . One disabled from duty by sickness may pray for health that he may do his work; or one hemmed in by internal impediments may pray for utterance, that he may serve better the truth and the right; or, if we have a besetting sin, we may pray to be delivered from it, in order to serve God and man, and not be ourselves left to Satan to mislead and destroy. But the answer to prayer may be, as it was to Paul, not the removal of the thorn, but, instead, a growing insight into its meaning and value. The voice of God in our soul may show us that His strength will enable us to bear it.

J. F. CLARKE

It is a test of prayer having attained its object when the praying soul feels there is no need to wrestle longer, and the sweet assurance is borne in that God has received our supplication.

F. B. MEYER

And I will pray the Father, and He shall give you another Comforter, that He may abide with you for ever. Even the Spirit of truth, whom the world cannot receive.

J O H N   1 4 : 1 6 ,   1 7

As the atmosphere stands between us and the sun, the transparent element through which we behold its brightness, and through which its warmth is transmitted to us, so the Holy Ghost mediates between us and Christ. "He shall take of Mine and shall show it unto you," says Jesus. Here is one side—the communication of the life and love and joy of the Lord to us. "The Spirit maketh intercession for us." Here is the other side—the communication of our needs and sorrows, our praises and confessions to the Lord. And both these ideas are involved in full communion with Christ.

A. J. GORDON

The Holy Spirit abiding in us makes fellowship with Christ a blessed reality. There is actual communication between Christ and us. He speaks to us, and we speak to Him. The Spirit brings to us the things of God from His heart, and He also brings the things of our heart to God.

Cause me to know the way wherein I should walk.

PSALM 143:8

To ascertain the Lord's will we ought to use scriptural means. Prayer, the Word of God, and His Spirit should be united together. We should go to God repeatedly in prayer, and ask Him to teach us by His Spirit through His Word. For if we should think that His Spirit led us to do so and so, because certain facts are said to be so and so, and yet His Word is opposed to the step which we are going to take, we should be deceiving ourselves. . . . No situation, no business will be given me by God in which I have not time enough to care about my soul. Therefore, however outward circumstances may appear, it can only be considered as permitted of God, to prove the genuineness of my love, faith, and obedience, but by no means as the leading of His providence to induce me to act contrary to His will.

GEORGE MÜLLER

God's voice in His Word, and His voice in the leadings of His providence never contradict each other. If the event points one way and the Word another we may be assured God is not speaking in the event.

Make me to understand the way of Thy precepts.

PSALM 119:27

*G*ive me a deep insight into the practical meaning of Thy Word; let me get a clear idea of the
tone and tenor of Thy law. Blind obedience has but
small beauty; God would have us follow Him with our
eyes open. To obey the letter of the Word is all the
ignorant can hope for; if we wish to keep God's precepts in their spirit we must come to an understanding
of them, and that can be gained nowhere but at the
Lord's hands. Our understanding needs enlightenment and direction; he who made our understanding
must also make us understand. It is to be noted that the
Psalmist is not anxious to understand the prophecies,
but the precepts, and he is not concerned about the
subtleties of the law, but the commonplaces and
everyday rules of it.

C. H. SPURGEON

"Howbeit when He, the Spirit of truth, is come, He will
guide you into all truth: for He shall not speak of
Himself; but whatsoever He shall hear, that shall he
speak: and He will show you things to come" John 16:13.

And He doeth according to His will
in the army of heaven, and among the inhabitants
of the earth: and none can stay His hand, or
say unto Him, What doest Thou.

D A N I E L   4 : 3 5

Natural law, the hand of God! Yes! I unquestioningly admit that the answers to prayer come generally along lines which we recognize as natural law, and would perhaps always be found along those lines if our knowledge of natural law were complete.

Prayer is to me the quick and instant recognition that all law is God's will, and all nature is in God's hand, and that all our welfare lies in linking ourselves with His will and placing ourselves in His hand through all the operations of the world and life and time.

R. F. HORTON

Prayer brings the soul under the operation of the highest laws. We call those laws spiritual, but they are God's natural laws in a spiritual world. Prayer is as necessary to certain results in the spiritual world as gravitation is to certain results in the natural world. If we have no regard for the spiritual law we shall certainly suffer.

I will lift up mine eyes unto the hills,
from whence cometh my help. My help cometh from
the Lord, which made heaven and earth.

P S A L M 1 2 1 : 1 , 2

*G*od's help does not for the most part, come
miraculously or obviously. It steals as gradually into our life as the grass of spring clothes the hills
with fresh and verdant robes. Before men can say, "Lo,
here! or lo, there!" it has suddenly entered into our
need and met it. A smile, a flower . . . a burst of music,
the picture of a bit of mountain scenery, a book, the
coming of a friend—such are the ways in which God
comes to our help. Not helping us far in advance, but
just for one moment at a time. Not giving us a store of
strength to make us proud, but supplying our need as
the occasion comes.

F. B. M E Y E R

Study well Psalm 121, and be assured of the Lord's
care of thee, and be encouraged to look to Him in
every time of need for grace to help thee. Then trust
Him to send the help in His own wise and loving way.
"God will take care of thee, be not afraid."

*Ask Me of things to come concerning My sons, and
concerning the work of My hands command ye Me.*

ISAIAH 45:11

*H*ow often during His earthly life did Jesus
put men in a position to command Him!
When entering Jericho, He stood still and said to the
blind beggars, "What will ye that I should do unto
you?" It was as though He said, I am yours to command. And can we ever forget how He yielded to the
Syrophenician woman the key to His resources, and
told her to help herself even as she would? . . . He
seems to set us beside Himself on His throne, and says
while the fire of the Spirit is scorching and ridding us
of sordid and selfish desire, all My resources are at
your command to accomplish anything which you
have set your hearts upon. Whatsoever ye shall ask that
will I do.

With the single limitation that our biddings must
concern His sons, and the work of His hands, and
must be included in the word of promise. Jehovah says
to us, His redeemed children in Jesus Christ,
"Command ye Me."

F. B. MEYER

Hear my prayer, O God;
give ear to the words of my mouth.

P S A L M   5 4 : 2

*T*his has ever been the defense of saints. As long as God has an open ear we cannot be shut up in trouble. All other weapons may be useless, but all-prayer is evermore available. No enemy can spike this gun. Vocal prayer helps the suppliant, and we keep our minds more fully awake when we can use our tongues as well as our hearts. But what is prayer if God hear not? It is all one whether we babble nonsense or plead arguments if our God grant us not a hearing. When his case had become dangerous, David could not afford to pray out of mere custom; he must succeed in his pleadings, or become the prey of his adversary.

C .   H .   S P U R G E O N

"No enemy can spike this gun." And yet how constantly the great enemy of our souls will attempt to. But let the Devil do his worst, we can still pray if we will. Have you been tempted to give up praying? If so begin to pray more earnestly than ever. If this gun is spiked it will be by our own decision not to pray more than by anything else.

*Without ceasing I make mention of you
always in my prayers; making request, if by any
means I might have a prosperous journey by the will
of God to come unto you.*

R O M A N S   1 : 9 ,   1 0

Pray though the gifts you ask for
May never comfort your fears,
May never repay your pleading;
Yet pray, and with hopeful tears,
An answer—not that you sought for,
But diviner—will come one day:
You eyes are too dim to see it;
Yet strive and wait and pray.

A D E L A I D E A . P R O C T O R

*P*aul's journey to Rome was not at all such a journey as he hoped to make, nor was his stay in Rome such as he had anticipated, yet how abundantly were his prayers answered in the blessing God made him to others in the journey, and while at Rome. So the answer to your prayers may be diviner than you sought for. Let God choose it. Not only so but learn to leave the working out of your life plan in God's hands. If your plans are defeated believe that God's plans are better than yours, and will result in the fullest answer to your prayers.

And the Lord descended in the cloud, and stood with him there, and proclaimed the name of the Lord.

E X O D U S   3 4 : 5

❋

*T*he answers to our prayers for spiritual vision may not always come as we expect. But, however, they come, come they will. None of those who wait for Him shall be ashamed. He will satisfy desires which He has Himself implanted. The King will be punctual to enter to see the guests who have complied with his conditions. As to Fletcher of Madeley, to Catherine of Siena, to President Edwards, to Dr. Payson, and to hundreds besides, so to you, when least expecting it, will come the beatific vision, perhaps constraining you to cry, as John Tennant did: "Hold, Lord, it is enough! or the frail vessel will break beneath the weight of glory."

F. B. MEYER

Have you had your vision of God yet as Moses did, as Isaiah did (Isaiah 6), as the three disciples did (Matthew 17:1-5)? Our prayer has not reached its zenith till we have our vision of God also. When the vision comes be not disobedient to the message it brings.

For this I besought the Lord thrice,
that it might depart from me. And He said
unto me, My grace is sufficient for thee.
2   C O R I N T H I A N S   1 2 : 8 ,   9

*G*od sometimes answers prayer by giving something better than we ask. An affectionate father on earth often does this. The child says, Father, give me this fruit. No, my child, the father replies, but here is bread, which is better for you. There was given to Paul a thorn in the flesh, a messenger of Satan to buffet him. In bitterness of heart, he cried, "Lord, let this depart from me." No answer came. Again he prayed the same words. No answer still. A third time he knelt, and now the answer came, not as he expected. The thorn is not plucked away, the messenger of Satan is not driven back to hell; but Jesus says, "My grace is sufficient for thee, for My strength is made perfect in weakness." Ah, this is something better than he asked, and better than he thought. . . . Dear praying believers, be of good cheer, God will either give you what you ask or something far better.

R .   M .   M c C H E Y N E

The Lord hath heard my supplications.

PSALM 6:9

he Holy Spirit had wrought into the Psalmist's mind the confidence that his prayer was heard. This is frequently the privilege of the saints. Praying the prayer of faith, they are often infallibly assured that they have prevailed with God. We read of Luther that, having on one occasion wrestled hard with God in prayer, he came leaping out of his closet crying, *"Vicimus, vicimus"*; that is, "We have conquered, we have prevailed with God." Assured confidence is no idle dream, for when the Holy Ghost bestows it upon us, we know its reality, and could not doubt it, even though all men should deride our boldness.

C. H. SPURGEON

A remembrance of past answers to prayer in our own experience will help strengthen our confidence that we are heard in our present supplications. It is well for us to frequently call to mind the many occasions in which our prayers have been abundantly answered. Not only so but with the Psalmist let us publicly testify that the Lord hath heard our prayers.

*And it shall come to pass, that before they call, I will
answer; and while they are yet speaking, I will hear.*

I S A I A H   6 5 : 2 4

*T*he answer to your prayers may be nearer than
you think. It may already have started . . . . On
the wings of every moment it is hastening toward you.
God will answer you, and that right early.

F. B. M E Y E R

The blessing is all prepared; He is not only willing but
most anxious to give them what they ask; everlasting
love burns with the longing desire to reveal itself fully
to its beloved, and to satisfy their needs. God will not
delay one moment longer than is absolutely necessary.
He will do all in His power to hasten and speed the
answer.

A N D R E W   M U R R A Y

Read and study Daniel 9:1-23, as illustrating the way
in which God speedily answers prayer. See also Acts
10. In each instance the answer to the prayer was being
made ready while the petition was being presented.
How precious the truth that God's answers are often
ready waiting for us to pray.

Verily, verily, I say unto you, Whatsoever ye shall ask the Father in My name, He will give it you.

JOHN 16:23

The Master says: Only pray in My name; whatsoever ye ask will be given. Heaven is set open to you; the treasures and power of the world of spirit are placed at your disposal on behalf of men around you. O come, and let us learn to pray in the name of Jesus. As to the disciples, He says to us, "Hitherto ye have not asked in My name: ask, and ye shall receive." Let each disciple of Jesus seek to avail himself of the rights of his royal priesthood, and use the power placed at his disposal for his circle and his work. Let Christians awake and hear the message: your prayer can obtain what otherwise will be withheld, can accomplish what otherwise remains undone.

ANDREW MURRAY

If this be so, how great the responsibility resting upon us in the matter of prayer. If we fail to pray, some soul will lose a blessing, some service will remain unperformed.

And the Lord said unto Joshua, Fear them not:
for I have delivered them into thine hand; there shall
not a man of them stand before thee.

J O S H U A 1 0 : 8

*T*his promise was followed by such praying, and such tremendous earnestness, and marvellous results as have seldom been equalled. The day this promise was made Joshua prayed that the sun might stand still upon Gideon, and the moon in the valley of Ajalon. And it is written, "And there was no day like that before it or after it, that the Lord hearkened unto the voice of a man: for the Lord fought for Israel." Verse 14.

What a day of prayer, and zeal, and victory all along the line, that will be in our lives when at the beginning of it some promise of God's presence and power, some promise of divinely given success and triumph shines out clearly before our soul's apprehension and faith! What can inspire to such bold and confident praying, such intense earnestness, patient endurance, courageous resistance, diligent aggressiveness, like a promise that makes a victory certain?

C H A R L E S A . C O O K

*God is faithful, by whom ye were called unto the
fellowship of His Son Jesus Christ our Lord.*

1 C O R I N T H I A N S   1 : 9

*I*n prayer there is not only the worship of a king,
but fellowship as of a child with God. Christians
take far too little time in fellowship. They think prayer
is just coming with their petitions. If Christ is to make
me what I am to be, I must tarry in fellowship with
God. If God is to let His love enter in and shine and
burn through my heart, I must take time to be with
Him. The smith puts his rod into the fire. If he leaves
it there but a short time it does not become red hot. . . .
So if we are to get the fire of God's holiness and love
and power we must take more time with God in fellowship. That was what gave men like Abraham and
Moses their strength. They were men who were separated to a fellowship with God, and the living God
made them strong.

A N D R E W   M U R R A Y

God's fires of love haven't much chance with some
souls; they do not remain long enough under the
power of that love to become heated through and
through.

*Oh Thou that hearest prayer,
unto Thee shall all flesh come.*

P S A L M   6 5 : 2

*W*hen we are asked why men should pray, and how prayer avails, we are not careful to answer more than this: "Prayer is the instinct of the religious life; it is one of the first principles of the spiritual world." It is clearly taught in the Word of God to be prevalent with the Almighty. It has been practiced by the noblest and saintliest of men, who have testified to its certain efficacy. Our Lord Jesus not only practiced it, but proclaimed its value in words which have been plunged a myriad times into the crucible of experience, and are as true today as ever! "Ask, and it shall be given you; seek, and ye shall find; knock, and it shall be opened unto you." We are content, therefore, to pray, though we are as ignorant of the philosophy of the *modus operandi* of prayer as we are of any natural law. We find it no dreamy revery or sweet sentimentality, but a practical living force.

F. B. M E Y E R

What prayer has been to men, should have more weight to move us to pray than the mystery of it has to keep us from praying.

Your heart shall live that seek God.

P S A L M 6 9 : 3 2

*W*ho that has prayed diligently, and experienced an answer, does not know that that one experience has done more for the life of religion in his or her soul than a great deal of reading or thinking? That consciousness of our relation to God is a thing which will develop through all eternity; but it has its beginning here, and the reason why God makes things depend upon our asking for them is that we may be thus educated into such personal intercourse with Him that that truth of sonship may never be merged and lost as it is merged and lost in all that direction of life which, unconsecrated by prayer, moves away from God.

C . G O R E

The manifold blessedness of prayer should stir the heart to greater diligence in it, until the prayer-life shall powerfully mould all thought and action, and it is proved by a glad experience that they live—live with an abounding life—that seek God.

Are you not daily proving the blessedness of prayer in your life, and if so will you not help others to know its blessedness as you do?

Pray to thy Father.

MATTHEW 6 : 6

So I prayed to the God of heaven.

NEHEMIAH 2 : 4

*M*uch so-called prayer is not to God. There is very little thought of God in it. We think of the audience, we think it may be of our need, but there is not a clear, deep sense that we have come into the presence of the all-holy, almighty, all-loving One, and are laying hold upon Him for His help. This is one of the most frequent causes of failure in prayer. We do not really pray to God. The first thing to do when we pray is to actually come into God's presence, to dismiss from our minds, as far as possible, all thought of our surroundings and look to the Spirit to present God to our minds and make Him real to us. It is possible by the Holy Spirit's aid to have God so really present that it almost seems as if we could see and touch Him.

R. A. TORREY

How true it is that our need, our weakness, our surroundings, our thoughts are often more to us in the time of prayer than God is. Let us seek a deeper consciousness of God in prayer.

*And this is the boldness which we have toward Him,
that if we ask anything according to His
will He heareth us.*

1   J O H N   5 : 2 4 ,   R . V .

*J*ohn supposes that when we pray, we first find out if our prayers are according to the will of God. They may be according to God's will, and yet not come at once or without the persevering prayer of faith. It is to give us courage thus to persevere and to be strong in faith as He tells us. This gives us boldness or confidence in prayer: if we ask anything according to His will, He heareth us. It is evident that if it be a matter of uncertainty to us whether our petitions be according to His will, we cannot have the comfort of what He says, "We know that we have the petitions which we have asked of Him."

A N D R E W   M U R R A Y

Make out a list of those things you know are according to the will of God. It is His will that we should be filled with the Holy Spirit, be sanctified—rejoice, grow in grace, that the church be pure, that sinners should be saved, that the Gospel should be preached everywhere, etc., etc.

But David encouraged himself in the Lord his God.

1 S A M U E L 3 0 : 6

And David inquired of the Lord.

2 S A M U E L 5 : 1 9

*E*vidently this was the holy practice of his life: to wait on God, quelling the fever of his soul, and compelling the crowd of impetuous thoughts to be in abeyance until time had been given for the clear disclosure of the divine purpose and plan. Like a child that dares not take one step alone, like a traveller in a strange country who is utterly dependent on his guide, so David lifted up his soul for the supreme direction which God only can give; to whom the future is as clearly defined as the past, and from whom no secrets can be hid.

F. B. MEYER

Thou hast sought advice from thy friends, and some have advised one course, and some another, and thou knowest not what to do. Thou hast tried this plan and that and failed. But hast thou sincerely, in a teachable spirit, with a willingness to do His will, inquired of the Lord? "If any man willeth to do His will he shall know."

Defraud ye not one the other,
except it be by consent for a season,
that ye may give yourselves unto prayer.
1   C O R I N T H I A N S   7 : 5 ,   R . V .

*T*he word used here ("give yourselves") occurs only three times in the New Testament. . . . It means literally to have spare time; to have leisure for anything, and to devote one's time to a thing. It teaches us that we are to take time for prayer, and to take time in prayer. Prayer is not only not to be omitted; it is not to be hurried. We are to approach God not only with a sober, but with a calm mind. Dew falls, we are told, only when the atmosphere is still, and the dew of prayer will fall abundantly on our souls only when we are at leisure. Have you to confess that in this busy age you have so much work to do that prayer is thrust into a corner? Then the lesson of this word for you is plain. Take a holiday. Do more by doing less. To pray well is to work well. Luther, a far busier man than any of us, used to say of his heavy days that he had so much to do, he could not do with less than two or three hours of prayer.

GEORGE C. H. MACGREGOR

Thou art near, O Lord;
and all thy commandments are truth.

P S A L M   1 1 9 : 1 5 1

*W*e should never leave our prayer-closets in the morning, without having concentrated our thoughts deeply and intensely on the fact of the actual presence of God; there with us, encompassing us, and filling the room as literally as it fills heaven itself. It may not lead to any distinct results at first; but as we make repeated efforts to realize the presence of God, it will become increasingly real to us. And, as the habit grows upon us—when alone in a room; or when treading the sward of some natural woodland temple; or when pacing the stony street; in the silence of night, or amid the teeming crowds of daylight—we shall often find ourselves whispering the words, "Thou art near; Thou art here, O Lord."

F. B. MEYER

And to the devout soul how true it is, "In Thy presence is fullness of joy." As the soul becomes flooded with a consciousness of God's presence it becomes also filled with a joy unspeakable and full of glory. In this joy of God's presence prayer becomes the sweetest converse of the soul with God.

When ye stand praying, forgive, if ye have aught against any: that your Father also which is in heaven may forgive your trespasses.

MARK   11:25

*A*cceptable prayer must imply that we are forgiven of God; for how can an unpardoned sinner hope to have influence with Him? But of nothing are we more plainly assured in the New Testament, and by the Saviour Himself, than that our own forgiveness by God is conditional upon our forgiveness of those who have injured us. The fifth petition of the Lord's Prayer significantly implies this, when it says, "Forgive us our debts as we forgive our debtors;" and, at the close of its record in Matthew, as if to enforce this particular thought more than any other, these words of Jesus are added: "For if ye forgive men their trespasses, your heavenly Father will forgive you; but if ye forgive not men their trespasses, neither will your Father forgive your trespasses."

WILLIAM W. PATTON

Read Matthew 18:23-35; Ephesians 4:32.

It ought to be easy to forgive when we remember how much we have been forgiven.

*From the end of the earth
will I cry unto Thee.*

P S A L M   6 1 : 2

*T*here may be an end to the earth, but there must not be an end to devotion. On creation's verge we may call upon God, for even there He is within call. No spot is too dreary, no condition too deplorable; whether it be the world's end or life's end, prayer is equally available. . . . David never dreamed of seeking any other god; he did not imagine the dominion of Jehovah to be local; he was at the end of the promised land, but he knew himself to be still in the territory of the Great King; to Him only does he address his petition.

C . H . S P U R G E O N

It is a great temptation when we are away from home, among strangers, to neglect prayer, or to give less time and real heart attention to it than when we are at home where we have our place of secret prayer. This is a danger we need to be watchful against. The vacation season at this time of year is often most perilous to the prayer-life, and unless we resolve that nothing shall interfere with our secret devotions we shall soon neglect them.

*Ye ask, and receive not, because ye ask amiss,
that ye may consume it upon your lusts.*

J A M E S   4 : 3

*H*ere is, in my judgment, the explanation of all unanswered prayer. When prayer is the voice of the self-life, the lust of the flesh, the lust of avarice, of ambition, of self-advantage, coming into the front, God will never heed it, for to heed it would be the worst thing for you and me. But, as I grow into Christ and come to know His thought, and as He grows into me and comes to subdue and control my thought, His will becomes my will, and the words of my prayer become the expression of His will and His word through me, and the Father hears the Son in the supplication of His disciple.

A. T. PIERSON

The prayer-life is not the self-life, but the Christ-life within the soul. What we need therefore for the fullest development of the prayer-life is, "None of self and all of Jesus." The question, "Am I asking for this to gratify my own pleasure?" will help us decide whether we are praying amiss.

*Yet the Lord will command
His lovingkindness in the daytime,
and in the night His song shall be with me,
and my prayer unto the God of my life.*

P S A L M   4 2 : 8

*H*ere may be seen that David's religion was a religion of prayer after deliverance, as well as before. The selfish who cry out in trouble will have done with their prayers when the trouble is over. With David it was the very reverse. Deliverance from trouble would strengthen his confidence in God, embolden his addresses to Him, and furnish him with new arguments. . . . There is great need of prayer after deliverance; for the time of deliverance is often a time of temptation, the soul being elated, and thrown off its guard. At such seasons much of the joy that is felt may be merely natural, as David's would probably be when rescued from that corroding care which injures the body as well as distresses the soul.

H E N R Y   M A R C H

Prayer after deliverance that has come in answer to prayer clinches the blessing that has come and makes it a permanent good to the soul.

And he said,
Oh let not the Lord be angry,
and I will speak yet but this once.
G E N E S I S   1 8 : 3 2

The nearer we get to God, the more conscious we are of our own unworthiness; just as the higher a bird flies in mid-heaven, the deeper will be the reflection of its snowy pinions in the placid mere beneath. Let the glow-worm vie with the meridian sun; let the dewdrop boast itself against the fullness of the ocean bed; let the babe vaunt its knowledge with the intelligence of a seraph—before the man who lives in touch with God shall think of taking any other position than that of lowliest humiliation and prostration in His presence. Before Him angels veil their faces, and the heavens are not clean in His sight. And is it not remarkable that our sense of weakness is one of our strongest claims and arguments with God. "He forgetteth not the cry of the humble."

F. B. MEYER

The man who prayed "God be merciful to me a sinner" went down to his house justified rather than the other. It is written, "He that humbleth himself shall be exalted."

My soul, wait thou only upon God;
for my expectation is from Him.

ometimes to go and be alone with God and Christ in the fellowship of the Spirit, just for the joy and blessedness of it; to open with reverent yet eager hands, the door into the presence chamber of the great King, and then to fall down before Him, it may be, in silent adoration; our very attitude an act of homage, our merely being there, through the motive that prompts it, being the testimony of our souls' love; to have our set-day hours of close communion, with which no other friends shall interfere, and which no other occupations may interrupt; to which we learn to look forward with a living gladness; on which we look back with satisfaction and peace; this indeed is prayer, for its own sake, for God's sake, for our friends' sake, for the church's sake, for our work's sake, prayer which we do not hurry through to still the conscience, but which (other things permitting) we can linger over to satisfy the heart.

BISHOP THOROLD

The soul has advanced in the prayer-life when such experiences are frequent.

Thy will be done in earth, as it is in heaven.

M A T T H E W   6 : 1 0

*C*ease meddling with God's plans and will. You touch anything of His and you mar the work. You may move the hands of a clock to suit you, but you do not change the time; so you may hurry the unfolding of God's will, but you harm and do not help His work. You can open a rosebud, but you spoil the flower. Leave all to Him. Hands down. Thy will, not mine.

S T E P H E N   M E R R I T T

> Take thou my hand, and lead me—
> Choose Thou my way;
> "Not as I will" O Father,
> Teach me to say;
> What though the storms may gather?
> Thou knowest best;
> Safe in Thy holy keeping,
> There would I rest.

Many who repeat the Lord's Prayer, and utter the words "Thy will be done" have no sincere desire in their hearts that God's will should be done in their lives. Indeed if their inner desires were revealed it would often be found that they wish above all things that their own will might be done, and not God's.

Without carefulness.

1 C O R I N T H I A N S 7 : 3 2

*W*hatsoever it is that presses thee, go tell thy Father; put over the matter into His hand, and so thou shalt be freed from that dividing, perplexing care that the world is full of. When thou art either to do or suffer anything, when thou art about any purpose or business, go tell God of it, and acquaint Him with it; yea burden Him with it, and thou hast done for matter of caring; no more care, but quiet, sweet diligence in thy duty, and dependence on Him for the carriage of thy matters.

R . L E I G H T O N

> Just to let thy Father do
> What He will;
> Just to know that He is true,
> And be still;
> Just to trust Him, this is all!
> Then the day will surely be
> Peaceful, whatsoe'er befall,
> Bright and blessed, calm and free.
> Just to follow hour by hour
> As He leadeth!
> Just to draw the moment's prayer—
> As it needeth.

F . R . H A V E R G A L

For the eyes of the Lord run to and fro throughout the whole earth, to show Himself strong in the behalf of them whose heart is perfect toward Him.

2 C H R O N I C L E S   1 6 : 9

Those who have made the deaf and dumb their study, tell us how much the power of speaking depends on that of hearing, and how the loss of hearing in children is followed by that of speaking too. This is true in a wider sense—as we hear, so we speak. This is true in the highest sense of our intercourse with God. To offer a prayer—to give utterance to certain wishes and to appeal to certain promises—is an easy thing and can be learned of man by human wisdom. But to pray in the Spirit, to speak words that read and touch God, that affect and influence the powers of the unseen world—such praying, such speaking depends entirely upon our hearing God's voice. Just as far as we listen to the voice and language that God speaks, we shall learn to speak in the voice and language that God hears.

A N D R E W   M U R R A Y

Nothing short of praying that prevails with God should ever satisfy our hearts.

*Peter therefore was kept in the prison; but prayer was
earnestly made by the church to God on his behalf.*

A C T S   1 2 : 5

*Elijah was a man of like nature with us; and he
prayed earnestly that it might not rain.*

J A M E S   5 : 1 7

The prayers of Scripture all glow with the white
heat of intensity. Remember how Jacob wrestled, and David panted and poured out his soul; the
importunity of the blind beggar, and the persistency
of the distracted mother; the strong crying and tears of
our Lord. In each case the whole being is gathered up,
as a stone into a Catapult, and hurled forth in vehe-
ment entreaty. Prayer is only answered for the glory of
Christ; but it is not answered unless it be accompanied
with such earnestness as will prove that the blessing
sought is really needed.

F. B. MEYER

Pray to be delivered from coldness and formality in
prayer. Be watchful against prayer drifting into a life-
less mechanical operation. It is the effectual fervent
prayer of a righteous man that availeth much.

In God I will praise His word, in God I have put my trust; I will not fear what flesh can do unto me.

P S A L M   5 6 : 4

*H*e who would keep up intimate converse with the Lord must habitually find in the Scriptures the highway of such companionship. God's aristocracy, His nobility, the princes of His realm, are not the wise, mighty, and highborn of earth, but often the poor, weak, despised of men, who abide in His presence, and devoutly commune with Him through His inspired Word.

Blessed are they who have thus learned to use the key which gives free access, not only to the King's Treasuries, but to the King Himself.

A. T. PIERSON
IN *GEORGE MÜLLER OF BRISTOL*

There is no fuel for prayer like the Word of God. When the fires on this altar burn low meditation upon the Word of God will be like fuel to make them flame up again. It is well to pray as we read, taking some thought suggested by the Scripture, some promise or some precept and incorporating it into our prayers. This will give variety in prayer and constantly enrich the soul.

But I have prayed for thee, that thy faith fail not.
LUKE 22:32

Let this mind be in you,
which was also in Christ Jesus.
PHILIPPIANS 2:5

*O*ur faith in the intercession of Jesus must not only be that He prays in our stead, when we do not or cannot pray, but that, as the Author of our life and our faith, He draws us on to pray in unison with Himself. Our prayer must be a work of faith in this sense too, that as we know that Jesus communicates His whole life in us, He also out of that prayerfulness which is His alone breathes into us our praying.

ANDREW MURRAY

As we are to seek to have Christ's mind in us in other things, His humility, His tenderness, His love, His patience, so we may seek His prayerfulness. It will help us to have His mind in prayer if we will try to make real to our hearts what must be the things for which He prays now as the Intercessor at God's right hand. Entering into fellowship with Him in this way will greatly stimulate our prayer-life.

Wilt thou not revive us again:
that thy people may rejoice in Thee?
PSALM 85:6

O Lord, revive Thy work in the midst of the years.
HABAKKUK 3:2

*T*he revival God is to give will be given in answer
to prayer. It must be asked and received direct
from God Himself. Those who know anything of the history of revivals will remember how often this has been proved—both larger and more local revivals have been distinctly traced to special prayer. In our own day there are numbers of congregations and missions where special or permanent revivals are—all glory be to God—connected with systematic believing prayer. The coming revival will be no exception. An extraordinary spirit of prayer, urging believers to much secret and united prayer, pressing them to "labor fervently" in their supplications, will be one of the surest signs of approaching showers and floods of blessing.

ANDREW MURRAY

Let us make our own hearts the first subject of this prayer, and then reach out to our own local church, and ever widen the circle till the whole Church of Jesus Christ is included.

The effectual fervent prayer
of a righteous man availeth much.

JAMES 5:16

*P*rayer has divided seas, rolled up flowing rivers, made flinty rocks gush into fountains, quenched flames of fire, muzzled lions, disarmed vipers and poisons, marshalled the stars against the wicked, stopped the course of the moon, arrested the rapid sun in its great race, burst open iron gates, recalled souls from eternity, conquered the strongest devils, commanded legions of angels down from heaven. Prayer has bridled and changed the raging passions of man, and routed and destroyed vast armies of proud, daring, blustering atheists. Prayer has brought one man from the bottom of the sea, and carried another in a chariot of fire to heaven; what has not prayer done!

AUTHOR UNKNOWN

What has accomplished so much for others, and through others, may accomplish much through us. Elijah was a man subject to like passions as we are, and so were others whose prayers have done mighty things. Pray! dear reader, pray! and be a means of blessing by prayer.

*Nevertheless we made our prayer unto our God,
and set a watch against them day and
night, because of them.*

N E H E M I A H 4 : 9

*T*here be many who appear to be mighty in prayer, wondrous in supplications; but then they require God to do what they can do themselves, and therefore, God does nothing at all for them. "I shall leave my camel untied," said an Arab once to Mahomet, "and trust to Providence." "Tie it up tight," said Mahomet, "and then trust to Providence." So you that say, "I will pray and trust my church, or my class, or my work to God's goodness," may rather hear the voice of experience and wisdom which says, "Do thy best; work as if all rested upon thy toil; as if thy own arm would bring thy salvation."

C. H. SPURGEON

Nehemiah was preeminently a man of prayer, but he was nonetheless a man of action. With him prayer and working, and prayer and watching were linked together, and his enemies were defeated in their evil designs, and his work was splendidly successful. Work for the thing for which you pray.

Wait on the Lord: be of good courage, and He shall strengthen thine heart: wait, I say, on the Lord.

PSALM 27:14

*G*od often delays the answer to prayer for wise reasons. The case of the Syrophenician woman will occur to you all. Matthew 15:21-28. How anxiously she cried, "Have mercy on me, O Lord, thou Son of David. But Jesus answered her not a word." Again and again she prayed and got no gracious answer. Her faith grows stronger by every refusal. She cried, she followed, she kneeled to Him, till Jesus could refuse no longer. "O woman, great is thy faith. Be it unto thee even as thou wilt." Dear praying people, "Continue in prayer, and watch in the same with thanksgiving." Do not be silenced by one refusal. Jesus invites importunity by delaying to answer. Ask, seek, knock. The promise may be long delayed but cannot come too late. . . . The praying souls beneath the Altar, in Revelation 6:9-11 seem to show the same truth, that the answers to a believer's prayers may, in the adorable wisdom of God, be delayed for a little season.

R. M. McCHEYNE

*Ye also helping together by prayer for us, that for the
gift bestowed upon us by the means of many persons
thanks may be given by many on our behalf.*

2   C O R I N T H I A N S   1 : 1 1

*G*enerally, if not uniformly, prayer is both starting-point and goal to every movement in
which are the elements of permanent progress.
Whenever the church is aroused and the world's
wickedness arrested, somebody has been praying. If
the secret history of all really spiritual advance could
be written and read, there would be found some intercessors who, like Job, Samuel, Daniel, Elijah, like Paul
and James, like Jonathan Edward, William Carey,
George Müller and Hudson Taylor, have been led to
shut themselves in the secret-place with God, and
have labored fervently in prayers. And, as the starting-
point is thus found in supplication and intercession, so
the final outcome must be that God's people shall have
learned to pray, if there is not to be rapid reaction and
disastrous relapse from the better conditions secured.

A .   T .   P I E R S O N

The blessings we secure through prayer are made
secure by prayer after they are received.

Unto Thee, O Lord, do I lift up my soul.

PSALM   86:4

That expresses the conscious effort to raise the psalmist's whole being above earth, to lift the heavy grossness of his nature, bound in the fetters of sense to this low world, up and up to the Most High who is his home. And can it be that that yearning and striving after communion shall go unsatisfied? Is it possible that I shall stretch out feeling hands and grope in vain for God? Is it possible that He shall not take note of me, that my poor faith shall be disappointed, that my prayer shall be lost in empty space, that my soul shall not find its Rest? Never. "What man is there of you, whom if his son ask bread, will he give him a stone?—How much more shall your Father, which is in heaven, give good things to them that ask Him."

ALEXANDER MACLAREN

"Behold the fowls of the air; for they sow not, neither do they reap, nor gather into barns; yet your heavenly Father feedeth them. Are ye not much better than they?"

"Surely goodness and mercy shall follow me all the days of my life."

*If ye abide in Me, and My words abide in you, ye
shall ask what ye will, and it shall be done unto you.*
J O H N   1 5 : 7

✻

*D*isciples of Christ! is it not becoming more
and more clear to us that while we have
been excusing our unanswered prayers, our impotence
in prayer, with a fancied submission to God's wisdom
and will, the real reason has been that our own feeble
life has been the cause of our feeble prayers? Nothing
can make strong men but the word coming to us from
God's mouth: by that we must live. It is the word of
Christ loved, lived in, abiding in us, becoming through
obedience and action part of our being, that makes us
one with Christ, that fits us spiritually for teaching, for
taking hold of God.

A N D R E W   M U R R A Y

His words abide in us only as we live according to
them. If we are obedient we shall eat the good of the
land. Isaiah 1:19

More and more some need to learn and remember
that a life of obedience to the will of God is the only
life that has any right to expect abundant blessings in
answer to prayer.

As the hart panteth after the water brooks,
so panteth my soul after Thee, O God.

P S A L M   4 2 : 1

*E*asiness of desire is a great enemy to the success of a good man's prayer. It must be an intent, zealous, busy, operative prayer. For consider what a huge indecency it is, that a man should speak to God for a thing that he values not. Our prayers upbraid our spirits, when we beg tamely for those things for which we ought to die; which are more precious than imperial sceptres, richer than the spoils of the sea, or the treasures of the Indian hills.

J E R E M Y   T A Y L O R

Prayer is the soul's sincere desire,
Uttered or expressed,
The motion of a hidden fire,
That trembles in the breast.
Prayer is the simplest form of speech,
That infant lips can try;
Prayer the sublimest strains that reach
The Majesty on high.
Prayer is the Christian's vital breath,
The Christian's native air,
His watchword at the gates of death
He enters heaven with prayer.

S E E   R O M A N S   1 0 : 1 ;   M A R K   1 1 : 2 4

For this shall every one that is godly pray unto Thee in a time when Thou mayest be found: surely in the floods of great waters they shall not come nigh unto him.

P S A L M 3 2 : 6

*R*emarkable answers to prayer very much quicken the prayerfulness of other godly persons. Where one man finds a golden nugget others feel inclined to dig. The benefit of our experience to others should reconcile us to it. No doubt the case of David has led thousands to seek the Lord with hopeful courage who, without such an instance to cheer them, might have died in despair. . . . The floods shall come, and the waves shall rage and toss themselves like Atlantic billows; whirlpools and waterspouts shall be on every hand, but the praying man shall be at a safe distance, most surely secured from every ill.

C. H. SPURGEON

This whole thirty-second Psalm is full of instruction, as showing how unhappy the soul becomes when sin keeps it from prayer, and as showing the blessedness of penitently praying and acknowledging one's sin before God. How true 1 John 1:9 is.

*But let him ask in faith,
nothing wavering.*

JAMES 1:6

*T*here is nothing so heart-searching as the prayer of faith. It teaches you to discover and confess, and give up everything that hinders the coming of the blessing; everything there may not be in accordance with the Father's will. It leads to closer fellowship with Him who alone can teach to pray, to a more entire surrender to draw nigh under no covering but that of the blood and the Spirit. It calls to a closer and more simple abiding in Christ alone.

ANDREW MURRAY

When the disciples became conscious of the need of faith they prayed for it. Faith is not natural and does not grow within us of itself. It is a fruit of the Spirit. Galatians 5:22. An increase of faith can come only through the Holy Spirit dwelling within us. Pray to be filled with the Spirit in order that you may have your faith increased. Then meditate much on the goodness and power of God and the promises He has given His children until your soul is filled with a firm, unwavering faith.

We have an Advocate with the Father,
Jesus Christ the righteous.

1   J O H N   2 : 1

The Father is always willing to give what Christ asks. The Spirit of Christ always teaches and influences us to offer the petitions which Christ ratifies and presents to the Father. To pray in Christ's name is therefore to be identified with Christ as our righteousness, and to be identified with Christ in our desires by the indwelling of the Holy Ghost. The Father Himself loveth us, and is willing to hear us: two intercessors, Christ, the Advocate above, and the Holy Ghost, the Advocate within, are the gifts of His love.

S A P H I R

The Godhead is engaged in helping us to pray. What a solemn yet blessed privilege to come into the circle of Divinity and be the Holy Spirit's mouthpiece in prayer.

What holier exercise can the soul engage in than that of prayer? In this more than in anything else the soul is lifted into the heavenlies. Never is the soul so engaged with the Father, the Son, and the Holy Spirit as in prayer.

Men ought always to pray.
L U K E   1 8 : 1

*P*rayer is reasonable and rational exercise of the soul. If we have a Father in heaven it is reasonable that we should come into touch with Him. . . . Not to go to God, your Father, in your need, not to ask His help, not to cultivate His friendship, not to keep the soul in fellowship with Him, not to pray, is to act irrationally to the last degree. A prayerless life is indefensible from any standpoint. A prayerless man is a monstrosity, a fit subject for our profoundest pity and commiseration. A poor soul who thus goes into self-imposed exile, consenting to the severance of all the ties which bind a soul to God, it goes without saying, is a spiritually impoverished soul; without God he is in the world.

S. G. HOWE

He who never prays lives in the outer circle of God's universe, farthest away from His throne. He who prays most lives in the innermost circle, nearest to God, where the light is the brightest and the glory the greatest. Which circle are you in?

But when ye pray, use not vain repetitions,
as the heathen do: for they think that they shall be
heard for their much speaking.

MATTHEW   6 : 7

*T*he best prayers are those which express, in simplest language, the simplest needs, trusts, and fidelities of the Christian soul. In all highest acts, thought must go along with feeling, and head with heart; yet it is communion of affection and desire in the worshipper, and not identity of opinion, that is the bond of worship. The church is chiefly and primarily a temple and an altar, not a school and platform: all its associations and services ought to appeal to the devotional nature. It is the atmosphere of prayer we ought to seek and find in the church; the vision and peace which come from communion with God; influences which draw out every devout and holy emotion, and quicken and nourish the eternal life in the soul.

J. HUNTER

It is in childlike simplicity that faith is most sweetly exercised, and prayer becomes most a matter of the heart. Come to God as a child to his father. Come not with elaborated lengthened petitions.

*Delight thyself also in the Lord; and He shall
give thee the desires of thine heart.*

P S A L M   3 7 : 4

*E*verywhere God works by law, by order, by
method. But our Lord taught us that prayer is
not the attempt to drag down the divine operations to
the level of our folly; prayer is a method by which we
lift up our will into correspondence with the methods
of God. There are stores of blessings which God
intends for us, but which He will not give unless we
energetically correspond with His law, with His
method, by prayer. Prayer is as fruitful a correspondence with the method of God as work—as fruitful and
as necessary.

C .   G O R E

We so often fail in our praying because we have
already prepared the track along which we want God's
blessing to come, whereas we should most sincerely
adjust our desires and our will to His will and His way
of blessing. It is well to ask as we begin to pray—Am I
in this matter delighting in the Lord, and fully surrendered to His will?

If ye then, being evil, know how to give
good gifts unto your children: how much more shall
your heavenly Father give the Holy Spirit
to them that ask Him?

L U K E   1 1 : 1 3

*T*he supreme gift of the Holy Spirit, which includes all real good, to be appreciated, and so to be of any value, must come to a longing of the soul itself. The asking expresses dependence, gives reality to faith, brings us near to God, renders the blessing more precious, and renders us the more grateful in the enjoyment of it. Through prayer we have immediate access to the fountain of spiritual life; and, since the will of God is our sanctification, if we fail to grow in grace, and to have spiritual power over the world, it is for lack of earnest, urgent, believing prayer.

J O S E P H   P .   T H O M P S O N

Have you received the Holy Spirit in fullness for holy living and efficient service? Ask and ye shall receive. We may test the value of our prayers by examining ourselves as to whether we are growing in grace and in spiritual power in the world.

I am crucified with Christ: nevertheless I live;
yet not I, but Christ liveth in me.
G A L A T I A N S   2 : 2 0

*C*hrist is our life"; "No longer I, but Christ liveth in me." The life in Him and the life in us is identical, one and the same. His life in heaven is an ever-praying life. When it descends and takes possession of us, it does not lose its character; in us too it is the ever-praying life—a life that without ceasing asks and receives from God. And this not as if there were two separate currents of prayer rising upward, one from Him and one from His people. No, but the substantial life-union is also prayer-union: what He prays passes through us; what we pray passes through Him.

A N D R E W   M U R R A Y

How watchful we need to be lest we hinder the flow of the divinely originated prayer current, and so rob our own souls and others also. The channels must be free from all obstructions. The soul must keep in accord with Christ in order that He may live in us in an ever-praying life.

Paul, a servant of Jesus Christ, called to be an apostle, separated unto the Gospel of God.

ROMANS 1 : 1

I ordained thee a prophet unto the nations.

JEREMIAH 1 : 5

Ask what thy work in the world is—that for which thou wast born, to which thou wast appointed, on account of which thou wast conceived in the creative thought of God. That there is a divine purpose in thy being is indubitable. Seek that thou mayest be permitted to realize it. And never doubt that thou hast been endowed with all the special aptitudes which that purpose may demand. God has formed thee for it, storing thy mind with all that He knew to be requisite for thy life work. It is thy part to elaborate and improve to the utmost the two talents which thou hast.

F. B. MEYER

A right exercise of prayer will prevent us from drifting through our life, and give purpose and definitions to our life's course, because through prayer we shall learn what God wants us to be and do, and shall direct our life accordingly.

*And the men took of their victuals, and asked not
counsel at the mouth of the Lord.*

J O S H U A   9 : 1 4

*I*n everything, the smallest and apparently clear-
est, consult God. This is the religious life, the
joyful life, the free life, to do nothing without the spirit
of prayer. There need not be any affectation of mere
posture and form of prayer; there is a spirit of fellowship, a continual realization of the divine presence, a
feeling after God; and then the uplifting of a hand is
prayer, as is the falling of a tear. When our reason
seems to be equal to the occasion, the temptation of
the Evil One is heavy upon us. We practically dismiss
God. . . . Joshua and his men were beguiled by appear-
ances by a most evident and obvious case. They took
not counsel at the mouth of the Lord, and what came
of it is revealed in the narrative.

J O S E P H   P A R K E R

The children of Israel accepted the appearance of the
bread of these Gibeonites as guaranteeing the truth of
their story without seeking to know the mind of the
Lord. The consequences of their neglect to consult
God should be a warning to all believers.

*Praying always with all prayer and
supplication in the Spirit.*

E P H E S I A N S   6 : 1 8

*W*hen next you are sensible of a mighty tide of desire rising up in your heart, bearing you forward in its bosom toward God, yield to it; let it have its blessed way with you. Though there be almost pain in the unutterable passion of desire, dare not to restrain it; for the Holy Spirit is then taking you up into the presence of God, and is leading you to ask those things which lie near His heart, and which brood over you as clouds of blessing ready to break. This is true prayer: the attempt on the part of man to tell out the deep, unutterable thoughts, which the Spirit is inspiring within.

F. B. MEYER

How gently yet how powerfully the Holy Spirit thus fills the soul with prayer! How watchful we should be for His promptings to pray, for when He prompts to pray the answer is certain. When we are not moved by a mighty tide of desire we should ask the Holy Spirit to create it, that we may ever pray in the Spirit.

I delight to do Thy will, O my God.

PSALM 40:8

*H*e who prays for divine help must not insult God by maintaining, at the same time, an attitude of opposition to Him. The second and third petitions of the Lord's prayer are: "Thy Kingdom come; Thy will be done on earth as it is in heaven." No prayer offered in a spirit inconsistent with this can hope to be accepted. Reason affirms this, and the Bible is explicit. Only the prayers of one who is truly consecrated to God can have power with Him. God is not a mere convenience, to be resorted to for selfish purposes in time of trouble. He invites us to enter into His spirit and plans, to identify ourselves with His cause and kingdom, to carry out our lives in His will, and He promises, on this condition, to care for us, and to hear our appeals for aid and blessing.

WILLIAM W. PATTON

No lesson is more important than learning to live in the will of God. Success in prayer depends upon it. See Romans 8:27. The Spirit's intercessions are according to the will of God, and we are to pray in the Spirit.

*And this I pray that your love may abound yet more
and more in knowledge and all judgment; that ye may
approve things that are excellent; that ye may be
sincere and without offence till the day of Christ;
being filled with the fruits of righteousness,
which are by Jesus Christ, unto the
glory and praise of God.*

P H I L I P P I A N S   1 : 9 – 1 1

*I*t is good to pray for one's friends. Indeed, the
friendship that does not pray is lacking in one
of its most sacred elements. We have also a good index
of the character of the friendship in the things that one
asks for one's friends. To seek for them only earthly
blessings is to miss friendship's highest privilege,
which is to call down heaven's benediction upon them.

It is interesting to study Paul's prayers for his
friends. His prayer for the Philippians may be taken as
an example. He does not ask that they may have more
of this world's good things, that they may be pros-
pered in business, but he asks for them those things
that will enrich their spiritual life and character.

J. R. MILLER

*Cast thy burden upon the Lord,
and He shall sustain thee: He shall never
suffer the righteous to be moved.*

P S A L M   5 5 : 2 2

"Thy burden" or what thy God lays upon thee, lay thou it "upon the Lord." His wisdom casts it upon thee; it is thy wisdom to cast it upon Him. He cast thy lot for thee; cast thy lot on Him. He gives thee thy portion of suffering; accept it with cheerful resignation, and then take it back to Him by thine assured confidence. He shall sustain thee! Thy bread shall be given thee; thy waters shall be sure. Abundant nourishment shall fit thee to bear all thy labors and trials. As thy days so shall thy strength be.

C. H. SPURGEON

Be sure, however, dear child of God, that when by prayer you cast your burden on the Lord, you leave it there, and do not go back to take up and carry thyself the load you have given to God to carry. In prayer learn to commit things to God. The definite promise that He will sustain us and that He will never suffer the righteous to be moved should greatly encourage us to cast all our care upon Him.

And the children of Israel saw the face of Moses,
that the skin of Moses' face shone.

EXODUS 34:35. READ ALSO
2 CORINTHIANS 3:18

*A*ll true prayer has a transfiguring influence. It brings us into the immediate presence of God. The holy of holies in the ancient temple, where the Shekinah was, was no holier than where you bow every time you pray. You are looking up into the face of Christ Himself. John was not nearer to Him, lying on His breast, than you are in your praying. One cannot thus look up into the face of Christ and not have some measure of transfiguration wrought in him.

Then prayer is the reaching up of the soul toward God. It lifts the life for the time into the highest, holiest frame. A prayerful spirit is full of aspirations for God. Its longings are pressing up Godward. No mood of spiritual life is more blessed than longing. It is God in the soul kindling its desires and yearnings for righteousness and holiness. It is the transfiguring of the spirit which purifies these dull earthly lives of ours, and changes them, little by little, into the divine image.

J. R. MILLER

*When ye pray, use not vain
repetitions as the heathen do.*
M A T T H E W   6 : 7

*B*ut earnest reiteration is not vain petition. The one is born of doubt; the other of faith. The prayer that springs from a deep-felt need, and will not cease till that need is supplied, may say the same things over a hundred times and yet they shall not be vain. Rather, as the same blood is repeatedly driven through the veins by the contraction and dilating of the heart, so all true prayer will flow forth over and over again, as the Spirit opens in yearning and closes itself in calm fruition on the grace it has received, and then dilates again in longing and sense of need. So the Master who warned us against the paganism of empty repetitions, enjoined upon us the importunity which prevails; and of Himself it is written, "And He left them and went away again the third time, saying the same words."

A L E X A N D E R   M A C L A R E N

Few men, if any, have been more mighty in prayer during the past century than George Müller of Bristol, and yet there were objects for which he continued to pray for years.

Let us not be desirous of vain glory.

GALATIANS 5:26

Nor of men sought we glory,
neither of you, nor yet of others.

1 THESSALONIANS 2:6

*E*njoyed much of the same spiritual sweetness which I felt last evening; but was much exercised on account of pride, or rather love of applause, which was excited by some approbation which I lately heard was bestowed on my preaching. Strove with all my might to be delivered from this hateful temper, and cried for some time to my Supporter and Strength ever to grant me His grace to help. Recalled to mind that I had nothing which I had not received; that I had most wickedly and shamefully wasted and neglected my talents; that the praise of men was of no worth compared with the approbation of God. By the divine blessing on these and other considerations, I was helped to overcome it.

EDWARD PAYSON'S JOURNAL

Learn like Jesus only to seek God's glory in prayer, and thou shalt become a true intercessor.

ANDREW MURRAY

But all these worketh that one and selfsame Spirit,
dividing to every man severally as he will.
1   C O R I N T H I A N S   1 2 : 1 1

He hath shown His people the power of His works.
P S A L M   1 1 1 : 6

The same Spirit who begets in the believer's heart the groanings that cannot be uttered, and the faith that takes hold on God with a firm grasp for the thing asked for, also works either in the realm of nature or the realm of grace to bring about the answer to prayer. And the obtaining or nonobtaining of answers to prayer does not depend at all upon the greatness or wondrousness of the things asked for, but rather upon the question whether or not the prayer and the corresponding faith have been begotten by the Holy Spirit.

D O U G A N   C L A R K

While the Spirit is working the prayer in our hearts, He is also working upon the hearts of men, or controlling their movements to bring about the answer. God's trains of prayer and events never miss connection, they are under one Dispatcher.

*And the king's servants said unto the king,
Behold, thy servants are ready to do whatsoever
my lord the king shall appoint.*

2 SAMUEL 15 : 15

*B*egin at once; before you venture away from this quiet moment, ask your King to take you wholly into His service, and place all the hours of this day quite simply at His disposal, and ask Him to make and keep you ready to do just exactly what He appoints. Never mind about tomorrow; one day at a time is enough. Try it today, and see if it is not a day of strange, almost curious peace so sweet that you will be only too thankful, when tomorrow comes, to ask Him to take it also—till it will become a blessed habit to hold yourself simply and "wholly at Thy commandment for any manner of service." . . . "Ready" implies something of preparation—not being taken by surprise. Let us ask Him to prepare us for all that He is preparing for us.

F. R. HAVERGAL

If we are not ready to do whatsoever He shall appoint, how can we expect Him to do what we request as we pray?

And she was a widow of about fourscore and four
years, which departed not from the temple, but served
God with fastings and prayers night and day.

L U K E   2 : 3 7

In fastings often.

2   C O R I N T H I A N S   1 1 : 2 7

*S*et apart this day for fasting and prayer. Was
unusually assisted in pleading for increase in
holiness. Felt such intense longings and thirstings after
more love to God and man, more devotedness to
God's will, more zeal for His glory, that my body was
overcome. Toward night was enabled to plead with
more fervency than ever, so that I trust this will prove
the most profitable day I have ever had. In the evening
was greatly assisted in prayer so that I could scarcely
retire to rest.

E D W A R D   P A Y S O N ' S   J O U R N A L

To the unspiritual fasting is not attractive, nor indeed
is it ever so to the flesh, but godly men have proven it
to be most helpful to the highest spiritual exercises.
Times specially set apart for fasting and prayer have
brought great blessings to others; why should they not
to us? Fasting and prayer are conducive to heart-
searching, and intensity of spiritual vision.

*And my soul shall be joyful in the Lord: it shall
rejoice in His salvation.*

P S A L M   3 5 : 9

Rejoice in the Lord always: and again I say, Rejoice.

P H I L I P P I A N S   4 : 4

*E*njoyed a very unusual degree of sweetness
and fervor this morning. O, how precious did
Christ appear to my soul! How I longed to be a pure
flame of fire in His service to be all zeal, and love, and
fervor! With what gratitude did I look up to Him, saying, Blessed Saviour, behold how happy I am! and to
Thee all my happiness is owing. But for Thee, I should
now have been lifting up my eyes, being in torments.
O, what shall I render unto the Lord for all His benefits! In the evening, in secret prayer, my soul was filled
with unutterable longings and insatiable thirstings after
God in Christ.

EDWARD PAYSON'S JOURNAL

Joyless praying must be heartless praying. If there is no
joy, it must be because the soul has not seen Jesus! On
the other hand how unspeakable the joy that fills the
soul to which there comes some new unfolding of the
glory of Christ while in prayer.

Thou shalt guide me with Thy counsel,
and afterward receive me to glory.

P S A L M   7 3 : 2 4

*P*rayer and faith, the universal remedies against every want, and every difficulty; and the nourishment of prayer and faith, God's holy Word, helped me over all the difficulties. I never remember, in all my Christian course, a period now (in March, 1895) of sixty-nine years and four months, that I ever sincerely and patiently sought to know the will of God by the teachings of the Holy Ghost, through the instrumentality of the Word of God, but I have been always directed rightly. But if honesty of heart, and uprightness before God were lacking, or if I did not patiently wait upon God for instruction, or if I preferred the counsel of my fellow-men to the declarations of the Word of the living God, I made great mistakes.

G E O R G E   M Ü L L E R

Answers to prayer are found only along the line of God's counsel. As we walk in the way of His will we shall receive rich answers to our prayers. How the testimony of this man of God should encourage us to perseverance in prayer.

I pray for them: I pray not for the world, but for them which Thou hast given me; for they are Thine.

JOHN 17:9

*J*ust like the Lord each believing intercessor has his own immediate circle for whom he first prays. Parents have their children; teachers, their pupils; pastors, their flocks; all workers, their special charge; all believers, those whose care lies upon their hearts. It is of great consequence that intercession should be personal, pointed and definite, and then our first prayer must always be that they may receive the Word. But this prayer will not avail unless with our Lord we say, "I have given them Thy word": it is this that gives us liberty and power in intercession for souls. Not only pray for them but speak to them. And when they have received the Word let us pray much for their being kept from the evil one, for their being sanctified through that Word.

ANDREW MURRAY

It is important that we speak to men about God: but it is vastly more important that we speak to God about men.

C. I. SCOFIELD

It is time for Thee, Lord, to work:
for they have made void Thy law.

P S A L M   1 1 9 : 1 2 6

*M*an's extremity, whether of need or sin, is God's opportunity. When the earth was without form and void, the Spirit came and moved upon the face of the waters; should He not come when society is returning to a like chaos? When Israel in Egypt were reduced to the lowest point, and it seemed that the covenant would be void, then Moses appeared and wrought mighty miracles; so, too, when the church of God is trampled down, and her message is derided, we may expect to see the hand of the Lord stretched out for the revival of religion, the defense of the truth, and the glorifying of the divine name. . . . How heartily may we pray the Lord to raise up new evangelists, to quicken those we already have, to set His whole church on fire, and to bring the world to His feet.

C . H . S P U R G E O N

It is ever a time for God to work, for without Him all our work is in vain. We may well pray at all times—"Let Thy work appear unto Thy servants."

Now when Daniel knew that the writing was signed, he went into his house; and his windows being open in his chamber toward Jerusalem, he kneeled upon his knees three times a day, and prayed, and gave thanks before his God, as he did aforetime.

DANIEL 6:10

*D*aniel was a very busy man. He was Grand Vizier of the Babylonian empire and had many and very important duties to perform. Jealous men were watching to detect the slightest mistake in his administration. But he found time to go aside three times every day for prayer and thanksgiving. Daniel was a most efficient official. His enemies were unable to charge him with any error or fault. Prayer through which men obtain wisdom and power from on high helps make men efficient. Busy men in responsible positions cannot afford to neglect prayer. Persecution did not turn Daniel aside from his prayer habit. Though it exposed him to the sentence of death he prayed and gave thanks as usual. Shame on us that we too often allow trifles to keep us from prayer.

CHARLES A. COOK

Arise, O Lord; let not man prevail.

PSALM 9:19

*P*rayers are the believer's weapons of war. When the battle is too hard for us, we call in our great ally, who, as it were, lies in ambush until faith gives the signal by crying out, "Arise, O Lord." Although our cause be all but lost, it shall soon be won again if the Almighty doth but bestir Himself. He will not suffer man to prevail over God, but with swift judgment will confound their gloryings. In the very sight of God the wicked will be punished, and He who is now all tenderness will have no bowels of compassion for them, since they had no tears of repentance when the day of grace endured.

C. H. SPURGEON

Have you tried the God of Israel? Your case is a peculiarly difficult and trying one. Your way is so completely hemmed in that no way of escape seems possible. It is as dark as it can be. But is anything too hard for the Lord? Have you tried the God of Israel? He is able to deliver thee. Ephesians 3:20.

I love the Lord, because He hath heard
my voice and my supplication.

P S A L M 1 1 6 : 1

*G*od often gives the very thing His children ask at the very time they ask it. You remember Hannah, 1 Samuel 1:10. She was in bitterness of soul, and prayed unto the Lord and wept sore. "Give unto Thine handmaid a man child." This was her request. And so she went in peace, and the God of Israel heard and granted her her petition that she had asked of Him, and she called the child's name Samuel, that is, "Asked of God." Oh, that you could write the same name upon all your gifts! You would have far more joy in them, and far larger blessings along with them. You remember David, in Psalm 138:3, "In the day when I cried Thou answeredst me." You remember Elijah, 1 Kings 17:21-23. You remember Daniel, Daniel 9:20, 21. Oh, what encouragement is here for those among you who, like Daniel, are greatly beloved—who study much in the books of God's Word, and who set your face unto the Lord to seek by prayer gifts for the church of God.

R. M. McCHEYNE

For thus saith the Lord unto the house of Israel,
Seek ye Me, and ye shall live.

A M O S   5 : 4

All practical power over sin and over men depends on closet communion. Those who abide in the secret place with God show themselves mighty to conquer evil, and strong to work and to war for God. They are the seers who read His secrets; they know His will; they are the meek whom He guides in judgment and teaches His way. They are His prophets, who speak for Him to others, and ever forecast things to come. They watch the signs of the times and discover His tokens and read His signals. We sometimes count as mystics those who, like Savonarola and Catherine of Siena, claim to have communications from God. . . . But may it not be that we stumble at these experiences because we do not have them ourselves? Have not many of these men and women proved by their lives that they were not mistaken, and that God has led them by a way that no other eye could trace?

A. T. PIERSON

God's promises give boldness to prayer, for His Word cannot fail.

O that my ways were directed
to keep Thy statutes!

PSALM 119:5

*D*ivine commands should direct us in the subject of our prayers. . . . We must ask the Lord to work our works in us, or we shall never work out His commandments. This verse is a sigh of regret because the psalmist feels that he has not kept the precepts diligently; it is a cry of weakness appealing for help to one who can aid; it is a request of bewilderment from one who has lost his way and would fain be directed in it, and it is a petition of faith from one who loves God, and trusts in Him for grace. Our ways are by nature opposed to the way of God, and must be turned by the Lord's direction in another direction from that which they originally take or they will lead us down to destruction.

C. H. SPURGEON

"Directed to keep." Yes, we need the Holy Spirit to direct us to keep the law of the Spirit, that we may not walk according to the flesh but according to the Spirit in all things. "Teach me to do Thy will; for Thou art my God. Thy Spirit is good; lead me into the land of uprightness."

*And He spake a parable unto them to this end, that
men ought always to pray, and not to faint.*

L U K E 1 8 : 1

*P*rayer which takes the fact that past prayers
have not yet been answered, as a reason for
languor, has already ceased to be the prayer of faith.
To the latter, the fact that prayers remain unanswered,
is only evidence that the moment of the answer is so
much nearer. From first to last, the lessons and example of our Lord all tell us that prayer which cannot persevere, and urge its plea unfortunately, and renew itself
again, and gather strength from every past petition is
not the prayer that will prevail. . . . For the individual
believer and above all, for every laborer in the Lord's
vineyard, the only way to gain spiritual power is by
secret waiting at the throne of God for the baptism of
the Holy Spirit.

W I L L I A M A R T H U R

Should we then pray for anything for which we cannot
pray perseveringly? Is not the fact, whenever it is a fact,
that we have no heart to pray for anything with importunity evidence that we should not pray for it at all?

Unto Thee will I cry, O Lord, my rock; be not
silent to me: lest, if Thou be silent to me, I become
like them that go down into the pit.

PSALM 28:1

M ere formalists may be content without answers to their prayers, but genuine suppliants cannot; they are not satisfied with the results of prayer itself in calming the mind and sub-duing the will—they must go further and obtain actual replies from heaven, or they cannot rest; and those replies they long to receive at once, if possible; they dread even a little of God's silence. God's voice is often so terrible that it shakes the wilderness; but His silence is equally full of awe to an eager suppliant; when God seems to close His ear, we must not therefore close our mouths, but rather cry with more earnestness; for when our note grows shrill with eagerness and grief, He will not long delay us a hearing.

C. H. SPURGEON

When we call up the central telephone office and there is no answer, we know there is something wrong somewhere. And when silence follows our praying something must be wrong, not with God but with us.

*Your Father knoweth what things ye have
need of, before ye ask Him.*

M A T T H E W   6 : 8

L ord, I know not what I ought to ask of Thee; Thou only knowest what we need; Thou lovest me better than I know how to love myself. O Father! give to Thy child that which he, himself, knows not how to ask. I dare not ask either for crosses or consolations; I simply present myself before Thee; I open my heart to Thee. Behold my needs which I know not myself; see, and do according to Thy tender mercy, smite or heal; depress me, or raise me up; I adore all Thy purposes without knowing them; I am silent; I offer myself in sacrifice; I yield myself to Thee; I would have no other desire than to accomplish Thy will. Teach me to pray; pray Thyself in me.

F E N E L O N

Yes, let Him choose thy way, thy blessings, thy sorrows, thy times. He knoweth what is best for me and thee. His infinite wisdom cooperating with His infinite love will keep Him from sending anything but the very blessing we most need when we allow Him to choose.

*But ye beloved, building up yourselves on your most
holy faith, praying in the Holy Spirit.*
J U D E 2 0 , R . V .

*W*hat our prayer avails, depends upon what
we are and what our life is. It is living in
the name of Christ that is the secret of praying in the
name of Christ; living in the Spirit that fits for praying
in the Spirit. It is abiding in Christ that gives the right
and power to ask what we will: the extent of the abiding is the exact measure of the power in prayer. It is the
Spirit dwelling within us that prays, not in words and
thoughts always, but in a breathing and a being deeper
than utterance. Just so much as there is of Christ's
Spirit in us, is there real prayer.

A N D R E W   M U R R A Y

It would be an anomaly indeed to pray in the Holy
Spirit, and at the same time live contrary to the Spirit.
It is the things that are contrary to the Spirit that hin-
der our praying in the Spirit. But he who lives in the
Spirit and does not fulfill the lusts of the flesh will have
access by the Spirit unto the Father.

This people draw near Me with their mouth,
and with their lips do honor Me, but have removed
their heart far from Me.

I S A I A H   2 9 : 1 3

W hy did we pray this morning? Do we often derive any other profit from prayer than that of satisfying convictions of conscience, of which we could not rid ourselves if we wished to do so, and which will not permit us to be at ease with ourselves, if all forms of prayer are abandoned? Perhaps even so slight a thing as the pain of resistance to the momentum of habit will be found to be the most distinct reason we can honestly give for having prayed yesterday or today.

A U S T I N   P H E L P S

David said, "I cried with my whole heart, hear me O Lord." Psalm 109:145. God wants the heart, the whole inner man, to go out to Him in prayer. He has no pleasure in the mechanical moving of the lips or the sounding of words while the heart is far away. As well might we adopt the prayer wheels of the priests of Tibet on which prayers are printed and left to be turned by the wind as to "say prayers" as a matter of habit.

*Now therefore, O our God, hear the prayer
of Thy servant, and his supplication, and cause
Thy face to shine upon Thy sanctuary that is
desolate, for the Lord's sake.*

D A N I E L   9 : 1 7

*T*here is no real incompatibility between the
unchangeableness of God, and His willingness to hear and answer prayer. The very condition
upon which He promises to give the things we need,
is that we ask Him. When therefore we bring ourselves
to the point of asking Him for the things we desire,
and when we receive them, it is not He that changes
His mind, but we change ours. We come to His terms,
we comply with His conditions, and He does precisely
what He has promised to do, without the slightest
change of purpose.

D O U G A N   C L A R K

When we pray along the line of God's promises, as
Daniel did, God's unchangeableness will be an inspiration to our prayers. The fact that the unchanging One
has purposed and promised to do a certain thing may
well stir us to pray that He may do it. Let us seek as
Daniel did to know just what God's purpose is, and
then pray accordingly.

Hear Thou from the heavens, even from Thy dwelling place, their prayer and their supplications, and maintain their cause, and forgive Thy people which have sinned against Thee.

2 C H R O N I C L E S   6 : 3 9 .   S E E
A L S O   V E R S E S   2 1   A N D   3 0 .

rayer supposes a full persuasion that God's Providence rules and governs all; that through all futurity His eye penetrates; that there are no events of our life in which He interposes not; that He knows the most secret motions of our hearts; and that to the hearts of all men He has access, by avenues unknown to us, and can turn them according to His pleasure. . . . It supposes a humble hope that as He knows our frame and remembers we are dust, He will not reject the supplications of the penitent returning sinner; that He is one who hath no pleasure in our sorrows and distress, but desires the happiness of His creatures, and beholds with complacency the humble and sincere worshipper.

H U G H   B L A I R

The Lord our God is a just and holy God, but He hath respect unto the lowly, and will not turn away the seeking soul. Isaiah 57:15.

Likewise the Spirit also helpeth our infirmities:
for we know not what we should pray for as we ought:
but the Spirit maketh intercession for us with
groanings which cannot be uttered.

R O M A N S   8 : 2 6

*F*irst of all, the Spirit awakens right desires and directs them to the proper objects; so that prayer goes straight to its mark. When not thus influenced, our desires are blind, being occasioned by mere natural impulse; and consequently they often long for objects which God cannot wisely bestow. But by the Spirit our desires are chastened, elevated, purified, and thus brought into sympathy with the divine plans, as respects ourselves and others. We are prepared to pray with a spiritual intelligence and intuition and to have a corresponding confidence awakened that we shall be heard.

W I L L I A M W. P A T T O N

How essential to the prayer-life it is that the believer should "be filled with the Spirit," Ephesians 5:18, and "walk in the Spirit," Galatians 5:16. Thus only can he pray "in the Spirit," Ephesians 6:18.

*Having therefore, brethren, boldness to enter
into the holiest by the blood of Jesus, by a new and
living way, which He hath consecrated for us through
the veil, that is to say, His flesh.*

H E B R E W S   1 0 : 1 9 ,   2 0

*C*hrist's presence at the Father's right hand, and His ministry in the Holy of Holies above, constitute the ground of our access there; and this blessed fact of our privilege to enter into the Holiest by the blood of Jesus is the truth with which the Epistle to the Hebrews is especially occupied. Indeed Christ's exaltation to the Father's throne is counted as our presence and residence there, and we find it so set forth in the epistles to the Ephesians, Colossians, and Philippians. But is it not plain that access carries with it the opposite idea of separation; that drawing near to God involves a withdrawing from fellowship with an evil world.

A . J . G O R D O N

The way of prayer is a highway of holiness, and no man can walk in that way while living in sin. He who would enter into the holiest must be cleansed. "Who shall ascend into the hill of the Lord? He that hath clean hands and a pure heart."

*Jesus also being baptized, and praying,
the heaven was opened.*

L U K E   3 : 2 1

*And in the morning, rising up a great while
before day, He went out, and departed into
a solitary place, and there prayed.*

M A R K   1 : 3 5 .   S E E   A L S O   L U K E
5 : 1 6 ;   6 : 1 2

*P*rayer in Christ on earth and in us cannot be two different things. Just as there is but one God, who is a Spirit, who hears prayer, there is but one spirit of acceptable prayer. When we realize what time Christ spent in prayer, and how the great events of His life were all connected with special prayer, we learn the necessity of absolute dependence on and unceasing direct communication with the heavenly world, if we are to live a heavenly life, or to exercise heavenly power around us. We see how foolish and fruitless the attempt must be to do work for God and heaven without in the first place in prayer getting the life and the power of heaven to possess us.

O my brother! if thou and I would be like Jesus, we must contemplate Jesus praying alone in the wilderness.

A N D R E W   M U R R A Y

*In every thing by prayer and supplication
with thanksgiving let your requests
be made known unto God.*

PHILIPPIANS 4:6

You have no kind of right to put the reign of law as an obstacle to prayer unless you are prepared to make the reign of law an obstacle to your doing anything to get your own living. . . . It is true that the man of prayer who approaches the Father in the name of the Son, in intelligent correspondence with the divine kingdom and divine purpose, draws out of the largeness of the love of God infinite stores of good things which God wills to give to him, and through him to his family, his church, his nation, humanity—stores of good things which are there in the providence of God waiting to comfort him, but will not be given except he prays.

C. GORE

The reign of law in nature stimulates to activity. The farmer sows his seed because those laws exist. So the reign of law in the spiritual world should inspire us to constant prayer. It is as necessary that we pray in order to get the blessing as it is that the farmer sow the seed to get the harvest.

Be still, and know that I am God.

P S A L M 4 6 : 1 0

In quietness and in confidence shall be your strength.

I S A I A H 3 0 : 1 5

*P*rayer is the peace of our spirit, the stillness of our thoughts, the evenness of our rec- ollection, the seat of our meditation, the rest of our cares, the calm of our tempest. Prayer is the issue of a quiet mind, of untroubled thoughts: it is the daughter of charity and the sister of meekness. He that prays to God with a troubled and discomposed spirit, is like him that retires into a battle to meditate, and sets up his closet in the out-quarters of an army, and chooses a frontier garrison to be wise in.

J E R E M Y T A Y L O R

Take time to get quiet before God. He has messages for thy soul, but how canst thou hear them if thy mind is preoccupied by many other things which trouble thee. Let the Lord Jesus speak peace to thy troubled Galilee. It was not in the storm of wind, nor in the earthquake, nor in the fire, that Elijah heard God's voice, but in the stillness that followed.

*I would seek unto God, and unto God
would I commit my cause.*

J O B   5 : 8

*In all thy ways acknowledge Him,
and He shall direct thy paths.*

P R O V E R B S   3 : 6

*L*ife is full of difficulties. The pointed spear
awaits the unwary at the bottom of the pit, the
top of which is covered by a slight film of earth. The
snare of the fowler, the pestilence that walketh in darkness, the net privily laid, the decoy bird, the Devil in the
wily serpent form—of these we need to beware. But
prayer is like the spear of Ithuriel; and before its touch
evil will be compelled to show itself in its native defor-
mity, so that we may be thrown instantly upon the
watch. Before entering into any alliance—taking a partner in life, going into business with another, yielding
assent to any proposition which involves confederation
with others—be sure and ask counsel at the mouth of
the Lord. He will assuredly answer by an irresistible
impulse—by the voice of a friend; by a circumstance
strange and unexpected; by a passage of Scripture. He
will choose His own messenger; but He will send a message.

F. B. Meyer

Be not anxious for your life what ye shall eat,
or what ye shall drink; nor for your body what ye shall
put on. Is not the life more than the food, and the
body than the raiment?

M ATTHEW   6 : 2 5

C ast all your care on God. See that all thy cares be such as thou canst cast on God, and then hold none back. Never brood over thyself; never stop short in thyself; but cast thy whole self, even this very care which distresseth thee, upon God. Be not anxious about little things, if thou wouldst learn to trust God with thine all. Act upon faith in little things; commit thy daily cares and anxieties to Him; and He will strengthen thy faith for any greater trials. Rather, give thy whole self into God's hands, and so trust Him to take care of thee in all lesser things, as being His, for His own sake, whose thou art.

E. B. P USEY

"Whose thou art." 1 Corinthians 6:19, 20. Acts 27:23. If thou art indeed God's own possession will He not take care of His own possession? Canst thou do better for thyself by consuming anxiety than by trusting all to Him whose thou art?

*And whatsoever ye shall ask in My name, that will
I do, that the Father may be glorified in the Son.*
JOHN 14:13

*T*hat the Father may be glorified in the Son.
It is to this end that Jesus on His throne in
glory will do all we ask in His name. Every answer to
prayer He gives will have this as its object: when there
is no prospect of this object being obtained, He will
not answer. It follows as a matter of course that this
must be with us, as with Jesus, the essential element
in our petitions; the glory of the Father must be the
aim and end, and the very soul and life of our
prayer. . . . Let us make His aim ours; let the glory of
the Father be the link between our asking and His
doing: such prayer must prevail.

ANDREW MURRAY

Here is a point where searching self-examination is
needed. Will the answer to my prayer glorify God? Is
that what I desire above all things in asking? Is self-
interest in any way influencing the character of my
praying? Prayer oftens remains unanswered because
we pray for something to consume upon our own
lusts, and do not aim purely at God's glory.

And when Moses was gone into the
Tabernacle of the Congregation to speak with Him,
then he heard the voice of one speaking unto him
from off the mercy seat that was upon the ark of
testimony, and He spake unto him.

NUMBERS 7 : 8 9

To keep in close touch with God in the secret chamber of His presence, is the great underlying purpose of prayer. To speak with God is a priceless privilege; but what shall be said of having and hearing Him speak with us! We can tell Him nothing He does not know; but He can tell us what no imagination has ever conceived, no research ever unveiled. The highest of all possible attainments is the knowledge of God, and this is the practical mode of His revelation of Himself. Even His holy Word needs to be read in the light of the closet if it is understood.

A. T. PIERSON

It is not our privilege to hear God's voice in the way that Moses heard it, and to see the light of God's presence over the mercy seat, but we may as really come into touch with God as he did. Let us not be satisfied with anything short of such fellowship.

*Evening and morning, and at noon, will I pray,
and cry aloud: and He shall hear my voice.*

P S A L M   5 5 : 1 7

*O*ften but none too often. Seasons of great
need call for frequent seasons of devotion. The three periods chosen are most fitting; to begin, continue, and end the day with God is supreme wisdom. Where time has naturally set up a boundary, there let us set up an altar-stone. The psalmist means that he will always pray; he will run a line of prayer right along the day, and track the sun with his petitions. Day and night he saw his enemies busy and therefore he would meet their activity by continuous prayer.

He is confident that he will prevail; he speaks as if he were already answered.

C .   H .   S P U R G E O N

There is no moment of our life when we do not need the help, guidance, protection which God alone can give. When our needs increase our prayers should multiply.

> I need Thee every hour,
> Stay Thou near by;
> Temptations lose their power
> When Thou art nigh.

And the people murmured against Moses, saying,
What shall we drink? And he cried unto the Lord.
E X O D U S   1 5 : 2 4 ,   2 5

*H*ow much better this than to rebuke the people, or to threaten to throw up his appointment, or to sit down in despondency as utterly out of heart! The disciples of John when they had buried their beloved leader, went and told Jesus. And in all ages the servants of God have been glad to turn from their discouragements and the ingratitude of those for whom they would gladly have laid down their lives, to Him whose heart is open to every moan, and whose love is over all, and through all, and in all. . . . Ah, fellow-workers, let us not carry the burdens of responsibilities arising out of His work. Our one thought should be to be on His track, and to be living in union with Himself. We may leave all the rest with Him.

F .   B .   M E Y E R

This is one of the greatest blessings and privileges of prayer, that we cast the burdens and perplexities that come to us in His work upon Him, and go forward in peace and joy.

Quicken Thou me according to Thy word.

PSALM 119:25

*I*t is well to know what to pray for—David seeks quickening; one would have thought that he would have asked for comfort or upraising, but he knew that these would come out of increased life, and therefore he sought that blessing which is the root of the rest. When a person is depressed in spirit, weak, and bent toward the ground, the main thing is to increase his stamina and put more life into him; then his spirit revives, and his body becomes erect. In reviving the life, the whole man is renewed.

C. H. SPURGEON

For nothing have we a clearer warrant for praying than for fullness of divine life. It is written, "I am come that they might have life, and that they might have it more abundantly." John 10:10. We may freely and believingly pray for that which Christ came to bestow. And if, as we open our hearts for the full inflow of that life, we receive it, all else that we need in our inner life will follow.

And he said, Let me go, for the day breaketh. And he said, I will not let thee go, except thou bless me.

GENESIS 32:26

*G*od often holds the suppliant in suspense for the sake of throwing him upon self-examination. It may be simply indispensable both for the good of the suppliant and for the honor of God, that he should be put to the deepest self-searching, to compel reflection and consideration for the purpose of convicting of some sin that must needs be seen, confessed, repented of and put utterly away. We must not overlook the great fact that when God grants signal blessings in answer to any man's prayer, it will be taken as a tacit endorsement on God's part of this man's spiritual state.

HENRY COWLES

While we hold on to God we must loosen our hold of sin. The hands of prayer must be empty or God cannot fill them with answers. Jacob had been grasping the things of the world, but now he is thoroughly in earnest in laying hold of God. He had come to an end of the self-life. He was to be no longer Jacob but Israel. We must have the same experience if we would prevail with God.

*And we know that all things work together for good
to them that love God, to them who are
called according to His purpose.*

R O M A N S   8 : 2 8

The Lord will perfect that which concerneth me.

P S A L M   1 3 8 : 8

*G*o for yourself, with all your temporal and
spiritual wants, to the Lord. Bring also the
necessities of your friends and relatives to the Lord.
Only make the trial, and you will perceive how able
and willing He is to help you. Should you, however,
not at once obtain answers to your prayers, be not dis-
couraged; but continue patiently, believingly, perseveringly to wait upon God: and as assuredly as that
which you ask would be for your real good, and therefore for the honor of the Lord; and as assuredly as you
ask it solely on the ground of the worthiness of the
Lord Jesus, so assuredly you will at last obtain the
blessing. I myself have had to wait upon God concerning certain matters for years, before I obtained
answers to my prayers; but at last they came.

G E O R G E   M Ü L L E R

The Lord is nigh unto all them that call upon Him, to all that call upon Him in truth. He will fulfil the desire of them that fear Him: He also will hear their cry, and will save them.

PSALM 145:18, 19

*T*he great point is, that we ask only for that which it would be for the glory of God to give to us; for that, and that alone, can be for our real good. But it is not enough that the thing for which we ask God be for His honor and glory, but we must, secondly, ask it in the name of the Lord Jesus, viz, expect it only on the ground of His merits and worthiness. Thirdly, we should believe that God is able and willing to give us what we ask Him for. Fourthly, we should continue in prayer till the blessing is granted; without fixing to God a time when, or the circumstances under which, He should give us the answer. Fifthly, we should, at the same time, look out for and expect an answer till it comes. If we pray in this way, we shall not only have answers, thousands of answers to our prayers; but our own souls will be greatly refreshed and invigorated in connection with these answers.

GEORGE MÜLLER

*Truly our fellowship is with the Father,
and with His Son Jesus Christ.*

1 J O H N   1 : 3

*I*n a world where there is so much to ruffle the spirit's plumes, how needful that entering into the secret of God's pavilion, which will alone bring it back to composure and peace! In a world where there is so much to sadden and depress, how blessed the communion with Him in whom is the one true source and fountain of all true gladness and abiding joy! In a world where so much is ever seeking to unhallow our spirits, to render them common and profane, how high the privilege of consecrating them anew in prayer to holiness and to God.

TRENCH

He who in prayer has not time in quietness of soul, and in full consciousness of its meaning to say Abba, Father has missed the best part of prayer.

ANDREW MURRAY

In the secret of His presence we obtain the sweet and effectual antidote for all the world's disturbing and poisoning influences. How precious and profitable the privilege of fellowship with Christ.

And Samuel said, Gather all Israel to Mizpeh,
and I will pray for you unto the Lord.

1 S A M U E L   7 : 5

*W*e often wonder at Luther, who spent three hours each day in prayer and meditation; at Bishop Andrews, spending the greater part of five hours every day in fellowship with God; at John Welsh, who thought that day ill spent which did not witness eight or ten hours of closet communion. It seems to us as if such prolonged praying must involve an endless monotony of vain repetitions. We forget that when men are sent to market with a host of commissions from their neighbors and friends, they must needs tarry longer than when they go only for themselves. It would be a very wholesome thing if the causes of others were to detain us more constantly before the Lord.

F. B. M E Y E R

Our prayer-life is not to be crowded into a corner, or treated as a secondary matter. It is to be developed, cultivated, strengthened, until gradually, yet certainly, it will fill a larger place, and bring richer blessings upon the church and the world.

*Ye have not chosen Me, but I have chosen you,
and ordained you, that ye should go and bring forth
fruit, and that your fruit should remain: that
whatsoever ye shall ask of the Father
in My name, He may give it you.*

J O H N   1 5 : 1 6

A merchant leaving his home and business,
gives his chief clerk a general power, by
which he can draw thousands of pounds in the merchant's name. The clerk does this, not for himself, but
only for the interest of the business. It is because the
merchant knows and trusts him as wholly devoted to
his interests and business that he dares put his name
and property at his command. When the Lord Jesus
went to heaven, He left His work, the management of
His kingdom on earth, in the hands of His servants.
He could not do otherwise than also give them His
name to draw all the supplies they needed for the due
conduct of His business.

A N D R E W   M U R R A Y

If such a privilege has been given us how foolish we
are if we do not take advantage of it to the utmost. The
signed check is given us; how foolish if we do not present it.

*And they gathered it every morning,
every man according to his eating.*

E X O D U S 1 6 : 2 1

*T*here is no time like the early morning hour for feeding on the flesh of Christ by communion with Him, and pondering His words. Once we lose that, the charm is broken by the intrusion of many things, though it may be they are all useful and necessary. You cannot remake the broken reflections of a lake swept by wind. How different is that day from all others, the early prime of which is surrendered to fellowship with Christ! Nor is it possible to live today on the gathered spoils of yesterday. Each man needs all that a new day can yield him of God's grace and comfort. It must be daily bread.

F. B. MEYER

Rise earlier to be more alone with Christ in the morning. Let neither the pressure of business, nor the allurements of pleasure, nor the tendencies of the flesh, nor the drowsiness of spirit, keep thee from thy morning interview and converse with the King of Kings.

Walk in the Spirit.

GALATIANS 5:16

For we walk by faith, not by sight.

2 CORINTHIANS 5:7

*Y*ou have accepted of Christ Jesus to make you whole, and give you strength to walk in new- ness of life; you have claimed the Holy Spirit to be in you the spirit of supplication and intercession; but do not wonder if your feelings are not all at once changed, or if your power of prayer does not come in the way you would like. It is a life of faith. By faith we receive the Holy Spirit and all His workings. Faith regards nei- ther sight nor feeling, but rests even when there appears to be no power to pray, in the assurance that the Spirit is praying in us as we bow quietly before God. He that thus waits in faith and honors the Holy Spirit and yields himself to Him, will soon find that prayer will begin to come.

ANDREW MURRAY

We walk by taking one step at a time; as we take one step after another in the Spirit, and in faith, we shall advance in the prayer-life. Therefore let us go forward steadily day by day ever learning some new lesson, ever reaching some new height.

Rejoice evermore. Pray without ceasing.
In everything give thanks: for this is the will
of God in Christ Jesus concerning you.

1   T H E S S A L O N I A N S   5 : 1 6 – 1 8

*I*t may be laid down as an axiom that whatever our Heavenly Father has promised us in His Word we may pray for, as we feel it to represent our needs. If Jesus has said, "Him that cometh to Me I will in no wise cast out," that is sufficient ground for one who has not found pardon, to ask and receive it. If the inspired apostle says, "This is the will of God, even your sanctification," the Christian may and ought to pray for sanctification. . . . If we are told that Jesus carried our sorrows as well as our sins, we should, in prayer give Him our sorrows as well as our sins. If we are told to cast all our care upon Him because He careth for us, we should do that thing. If we are commanded to "Rejoice evermore, pray without ceasing, in everything give thanks," we should pray for that state of mind and heart, in which God's grace may enable us to do so.

D O U G A N   C L A R K

If we would "rejoice evermore" there must be as much praising as praying.

The Spirit helpeth our infirmities.
R O M A N S   8 : 2 6

*N*ever do we feel them more than at the hour of prayer. Sometimes our thoughts scatter like a flock of sheep, or flag and faint before the spiritual effort of stirring ourselves up to take hold on God. Who does not have times, when (to use Jeremy Taylor's similitude) prayer is like the rise of a lark against an east wind? We even tire in maintaining the attitude of devotion; and how much more its spirit! We know not what to pray for; we are ignorant of the best arguments to employ; we ask amiss; we cannot keep in the perpetual spirit and temper of devotion; we lack that calm faith, which can leave its burden at the mercy-seat, and be at rest. In all this the Spirit helpeth us.

F. B. MEYER

And as the Holy Spirit dwelling within us, and working mightily overcomes all these infirmities what liberty, what confidence, what joy, what power we have in prayer! How thankful we should be that we have such an all-sufficient Helper in our prayer-life, and that therefore we need not fail in our praying.

Whoso stoppeth his ears at the cry of the poor,
he also shall cry himself, but shall not be heard.

P R O V E R B S 2 1 : 1 3

*M*any are saying, "The promises of God are not true. God does not hear my prayers." Has God ever promised to hear your prayers? God very plainly describes the class whose prayers He hears. Do you belong to that class? Are you listening to His words? (See Zechariah 7:11–13.) If not, He has distinctly said He will not listen to your prayers, and in not listening to you, He is simply keeping His word. . . . If we will not listen to the poor when they cry unto us in their need, God will not listen unto us when we cry unto Him in our need.

R . A . T O R R E Y

Our God often treats men as they treat Him. If we do not hearken unto Him He will not hearken unto us. If we do not obey Him He will not heed our cry. Proverbs 1:24, 25–28. We often refrain from hearing the cry of the poor because we say they are unworthy and undeserving, and will not make good use of our gifts. Suppose God should treat us that way, when would we ever receive anything from Him?

After this manner therefore pray ye.
MATTHEW 6 : 9

*I*n all His instructions, our Lord Jesus spoke much oftener to His disciples about their praying than their preaching. In the farewell discourse, He said little about preaching, but much about the Holy Spirit, and their asking whatsoever they would in His Name. If we are to return to this life of the first apostles and of Paul, and really accept the truth every day—my first work, my only strength is intercession, to secure the power of God on the souls entrusted to me—we must have the courage to confess past sin, and to believe that there is deliverance. To break through old habits, to resist the clamor of pressing duties that have always had their way, to make every other call subordinate to this one, whether others approve or not, will not be easy at first. But the men or women who are faithful will not only have a reward themselves, but become benefactors to their brethren.

ANDREW MURRAY

Nothing can atone for the loss of secret and direct intercourse with God.

Let, I pray Thee, Thy merciful kindness be for my comfort, according to Thy word unto Thy servant.

PSALM 119:76

*B*efore prayer, it is God's Word that prepares me for it, by revealing what the Father has bid me ask. In prayer, it is God's Word that strengthens me by giving my faith its warrant and its plea. And after prayer it is God's Word that brings me the answer when I have prayed, for in it the Spirit gives me to hear the Father's voice. Prayer is not monologue but dialogue; God's voice in response to mine is its most essential part. Listening to God's voice is the secret of the assurance that He will listen to mine.

ANDREW MURRAY

Our prayers are according to the mind of God when they are according to the Word of God.

C. H. SPURGEON

God speaks and we pray; we pray and God speaks. When we pray according to His Word, He will answer according to our word, that is, according to His own Word.

*For My thoughts are not your thoughts, neither are
your ways My ways, saith the Lord. For as the heavens
are higher than the earth, so are My ways higher than
your ways, and My thoughts than your thoughts.*

I S A I A H 5 5 : 8 , 9

he Bible recognizes various modes of divine
action in answering prayer. In the olden times,
when God was founding the true religion, and attest-
ing it by signs, evidently supernatural, and intended to
manifest His immediate presence and power, prayer
appeared to be answered, on many occasions, by
direct acts of God; at least no other agency seemed to
be employed. It was so, when, at the prayer of Jesus,
God raised Lazarus from the dead; when, at the request
of the centurion, the servant was healed immediately
and at a distance; and when after the earnest entreaty
of Elijah, fire came down and consumed the sacrifice
on Carmel. But, in other cases, God put natural causes
into motion, to secure the desired end. Exodus 10:18,
19; Isaiah 38:5-21.

W I L L I A M W. P A T T O N

For we are labourers together with God.

1   C O R I N T H I A N S   3 : 9

*T*here is the great secret of success. Work with all your might; but trust not the least in your work. Pray with all your might for the blessing of God; but work at the same time, with all diligence, with all patience, with all perseverance. Pray then and work. Work and pray. And still again pray and then work. And so on all the days of your life. The result will surely be abundant blessing. . . . Speak also for the Lord, as if everything depended on your exertions. Yet trust not the least in your exertions, but in the Lord, who alone can cause your efforts to be made effectual, to the benefit of your fellow-men or fellow-believers.

G E O R G E   M Ü L L E R

By prayer we join hands with God in His work and become co-workers with Him. Prayer connects our efforts with God's working and makes those efforts effectual. Prayer is the piston rod between the hidden power and the outer operation or activity. Praying is therefore part of the work; we are working when we pray, and we are praying when we work.

*Who in the days of his flesh, when he had offered
up prayers and supplications with strong crying and
tears unto Him that was able to save him from
death, and was heard in that he feared.*

HEBREWS 5 : 7

*I*n the afternoon God was with me of a truth.
Oh, it was blessed company indeed! God
enabled me so to agonize in prayer that I was quite wet
with sweat, though in the shade and cool wind. My
soul was drawn out very much for the world; I grasped
for multitudes of souls. I think I had more enlargement
for sinners than for the children of God, though I felt
as if I could spend my life in cries for both. I had great
enjoyment in communion with my dear Saviour. I
think I never in my life felt such an entire weanedness
from this world, and so much resigned to God in
everything. Oh that I may always live to and upon my
blessed God! Amen.

JOURNAL OF DAVID BRAINERD

Prayer need not always be an agonizing of soul, but
there may come times when we shall be moved so
mightily and be filled with such deep concern, that our
praying will be a moving of the soul to tears.

*And having an High Priest over the
house of God; let us draw near with a true heart
in full assurance of faith.*

H E B R E W S   1 0 : 2 1 ,   2 2

*I*n prayer, the soul approaches to the borders of an invisible world, and acts as a spirit holding intercourse with the Father of spirits. It drops for a time the remembrance of its earthly connections, to dwell among everlasting objects. Prayer, by this means, both composes and purifies the heart; it gives the soul its proper elevation toward God, and has a happy effect to counterwork the dangerous impression made by the corruptions of the world around us.

H U G H   B L A I R

"Let us draw near." It was a solemn time when on the great day of atonement the High Priest went into the most Holy Place, and stood in the presence of the Shekinah glory. That was the nearest to God any man then came. But now the veil has been rent and we are all priests unto God, and may draw near to God. "Draw nigh to God and He will draw nigh to you."

They that wait upon the Lord shall
renew their strength; they shall mount up with wings
as eagles; they shall run, and not be weary;
and they shall walk, and not faint.

I S A I A H   4 0 : 3 1

o wait upon God is to be silent that He may speak, expecting all things from Him, and girded for instant unquestioning obedience to the slightest movement of His will. That is waiting upon God. All the spiritual senses alive, alert, expectant; separated unto Him as His servant and soldier—waiting. It is not the waiting of an idler; it is not the waiting of a dreamer. It is the quiet waiting of one who is girt and ready, one who looks upon life as a battlefield and a sphere for service, who has one Master and but one, to whom he looks for everything, from whom alone he expects anything. This is waiting upon God according to the Scriptures.

C . I . S C O F I E L D

True prayer is much more than uttering words before God. It is bringing all the faculties of the mind and all the emotions of the heart into "attention" before God, as a regiment before a general.

Epaphras, who is one of you, a servant
of Christ, saluteth you, always labouring fervently
for you in prayers, that ye may stand perfect
and complete in all the will of God.

C O L O S S I A N S   4 : 1 2

*T*hese words represent a high water mark in the Bible teaching regarding prayer. The words "laboring fervently" might more literally be translated "agonizing," which is, perhaps, the strongest word that could be employed. Its meaning we cannot at once realize. It startles us, it pains us, at first it repels us. To speak of agony in connection with prayer might seem to some unwise. It might seem to ensure our turning from prayer. Yet there the word lies, written by the inspiration of the Spirit of God, and full of the deepest teaching about the manner of prayer. . . . We are to labor at prayer as a man labors at his daily work. We are to put forth our energy in this work until we are weary. Colossians 1:29. In our day the aim of some laborers seems to be to make their task as light as possible. It is to be feared that some of us labor in prayer after that fashion.

G E O R G E   H .   C .   M A C G R E G O R

Hear, O Lord, when I cry with my voice:
have mercy also upon me, and answer me.

P S A L M   2 7 : 7

As a good soldier, David knew how to handle his weapons, and found himself much at home with the weapon of "all prayer." Note his anxiety to be heard. Pharisees care not a fig for the Lord's hearing them, so long as they are heard of men, or cleanse their own pride with their sounding devotion; but with a genuine man, the Lord's ear is everything. The voice may be profitably used even at private prayer; for though it is unnecessary, it is often helpful, and aids in preventing distractions. . . . We may expect answers to prayer, and should not be easy without them any more than we should be if we had written a letter to a friend upon important business, and had received no reply.

C . H . S P U R G E O N

It is not the length of time we spend in prayer, as it is getting the ear of God in very deed, that tells in our praying. Quality rather than quantity is the essential thing in the prayer-life, as in many other things.

*I exhort therefore, that, first of all,
supplications, prayer, intercessions, and giving
of thanks, be made for all men; for kings and for all
that are in authority; that we may lead a quiet and
peaceable life in all godliness and honesty.*

1   T I M O T H Y   2 : 1 ,   2

*N*o sooner had God begun in Abraham to
form for Himself a people from whom
kings, yea the Great King, should come forth, than we
see what power the prayer of God's faithful servant
has to decide the destinies of those who come in contact with him. In Abraham we see how prayer is not
only, or even chiefly, the means of obtaining blessing
for ourselves, but is the exercise of his royal preroga-
tive to influence the destinies of men, and the will of
God which rules them. We do not once find Abraham
praying for himself. His prayer for Sodom and Lot, for
Abimelech, for Ishmael, prove what power a man who
is God's friend has to make the history of those
around him. As image-bearer and representative of
God on earth, redeemed man has by his prayers to
determine the history of this earth.

A N D R E W   M U R R A Y

Thou castest off fear,
and restrainest prayer before God.

J O B   1 5 : 4

My people have forsaken Me.

J E R E M I A H   2 : 1 3

*T*ake heed, then; watch and pray; examine yourselves whether ye be in the faith; prove your
ownselves! Expose yourselves to the searching light of
God's Spirit. Cultivate the honest and good heart.
Most of the infidelity of the present day arises from
man's disinclination to retain God in his knowledge.
More skepticism may be traced to a neglected prayer
closet than to the arguments of infidels or the halls of
secularists. First, men depart from God; then they
deny Him. And therefore for the most part unbelief
will not yield to clever sermons on the evidences but
to home thrusts that pierce the points of the harness
to the soul within.

F. B. M E Y E R

Praying is a great work, and therefore is not to be
entered upon as though it availed little. The great
movements of the church and of nations hinge on
prayer. Pray therefore for all men, for the whole wide
world.

*He which testifieth these things saith, Surely I come
quickly. Amen. Even so, come, Lord Jesus.*

R E V E L A T I O N   2 2 : 2 0

*I*n the inwardness of prayer we see its subjective
power, transforming the church into the likeness
of Christ. But we also see that prayer is an objective
power, mighty to accomplish. It is in no sense an effort
to change the will of God; but a taking hold in cooperation with Him, according to His own foreordained
plan to bring about what He wills. We see in Scripture,
that every great event has been brought forth by
prayer. So today, the ever-increasing volume of prayer
is the power that is propelling the ponderous wheels
of providence preparatory to the *parousia* of the Son of
man. The Advent will be the Lord Jesus given in
response to the prayer of His people; and it will also
be His reception of the church in answer to His own
prayer.

J .   A .   F R A S E R

It is ever timely, never more so than now, to pray the
prayer with which the inspired volume closes. "Even
so, come, Lord Jesus."

Let my prayer be set forth before Thee
as incense; and the lifting up of my hands as the
evening sacrifice. Set a watch, O Lord, before
my mouth; keep the door of my lips.

P S A L M   1 4 1 : 2 ,   3

An obedient mind will sometimes be led in prayer, as a blind man is led by his guide—in the right way, and yet unable to see the path or trace the footsteps. Oh, blessed privilege sometimes accorded to God's saints, to be so in the Spirit that thoughts come unbidden, language shapes itself, and desires breathe spontaneously, as though we were in the unbroken circuit between the throne and the footstool, and God's desires were only flowing through us and returning to Himself again.

A . J . G O R D O N

The incense was burned with fire from the altar of sacrifice, and that fire came from heaven. Incense is therefore a symbol of true prayer. It starts from God, and it goes to God. If the Holy Spirit keeps the door of our lips no prayer will issue therefrom but what He has first of all inspired.

Unto Thee have I opened my cause.

J E R E M I A H   2 0 : 1 2

*G*od always seemed nigh at hand. His ear always bent down to the least whisper of His servant's need. Compelled to live much alone, this much-suffering man (Jeremiah) acquired the habit of counting on the companionship of God as one of the undoubted facts of his life. He poured into the ear of God every thought as it passed through his soul. He spread forth his roots by the river of God, which is full of water. There was no fear therefore that his leaf would become sere in the summer heat, or that he would cease from yielding fruit in the year of drought. Let us seek this attitude of soul, which easily turns from man to God; not forgetting the hours of pro- longed fellowship, but, in addition, acquiring the habit of talking over our life with one who does not need to be informed of what transpires, but awaits with infinite desire to receive the confidence of His children. Talk over each detail of your life with God, telling Him all things, and finding the myriad needs of the soul satis- fied in Him.

F. B. MEYER

*O Lord my God, I cried unto Thee,
and Thou hast healed me.*

P S A L M 3 0 : 2

*D*avid sent up prayers for himself and for his people when visited with the pestilence. He went at once to headquarters, and not roundabout to fallible means. God is the best physician even for our bodily infirmities. We do very wickedly and foolishly when we forget God. It was sin in Asa that he trusted to physicians and not to God. If we must have a physician let it be so, but still let us go to our God first of all; and, above all, remember that there can be no power to heal in medicine of itself; the healing energy must flow from the divine hand. If our watch is out of order, we take it to the watchmaker; if body or soul be in an evil plight, let us resort to Him who created them, and has unfailing skill to put them in right condition.

C. H. SPURGEON

There is a wider realm for the exercise of prayer than we are wont to imagine. Surely our bodies which are temples of the Holy Ghost may well be taken to God in prayer when sickness befalls them.

Whatsoever ye do,
do all to the glory of God.

1   C O R I N T H I A N S   1 0 : 3 1

*W*hat a humbling thought that so often there is earnest prayer for a child or a friend, for a work or a circle, in which the thought of our joy or our pleasure was far stronger than any yearnings for God's glory. No wonder there are so many unanswered prayers; here we have the secret. God would not be glorified when that glory was not our object. He that would pray the prayer of faith will have to give himself to live literally so that the Father in all things may be glorified in him. This must be his aim; without this there cannot be the prayer of faith. "How can ye believe," said Jesus, "which receive glory of one another, and the glory that cometh from the only God ye seek not." All seeking of our own glory with men makes faith impossible; it is the deep, intense self-sacrifice that gives up its own glory, and seeks the glory of God alone, that wakens in the soul that spiritual susceptibility of the Divine, which is faith.

A N D R E W   M U R R A Y

What wilt thou Queen Esther?
And what is thy request? it shall be given thee
to the half of the kingdom.

E S T H E R   5 : 3

*D*ost thou want nothing, O, my fellow-mortal? Hast thou nothing to ask? Yes, thou repliest, I need an infinite supply. Well, then, draw near to thy precious King and Bridegroom without fear. Lo! He holds out His golden sceptre to thee, saying, "Only ask; not the half, but the whole of My kingdom shall be granted; nay, I will give Myself unto thee." Disclose to Him, therefore, thy whole heart, mentioning all thy wants and grievances. Whatever is poured out before Him, is lodged in its proper place; He takes the burden from thee, and encourages thee to hope for seasonable and full relief. . . . Ask of Him, therefore, all thou needest, and ask in faith.

C. H. V. BOGATSKY

There are many things which are not in harmony with the will of God, and for which therefore we may not pray; but what an endless list of blessings may be found in fullest harmony with the will of God, for which we may pray.

*Finally, brethren, pray for us, that the word
of the Lord may run and be glorified, even as also it is
with you, and that all may be delivered from
unreasonable and evil men.*

2 THESSALONIANS 3:1, 2

R.V.

*W*ho can say what power a church could develop and exercise, if it gave itself to the work of prayer day and night for the coming of the kingdom, for God's power on His servants and His Word, for the glorifying of God in the salvation of souls? Most churches think their members are gathered into one simply to take care of and build up each other. They know not that God rules the world by the prayers of His saints, that prayer is the power by which Satan is conquered, that by prayer the church on earth has disposal of the powers of the heavenly world. They do not remember that Jesus has, by His promise (Matthew 18:19, 20), consecrated every assembly in His name to be a gate of heaven, where His presence is to be felt, and His power experienced in the Father fulfilling their desires.

ANDREW MURRAY

Pray for your pastor and all ministers.

*Ask, and ye shall receive, that
your joy may be full.*
J O H N   1 6 : 2 4

*T*he lack of joy in Christian hearts may often be traced to a failure to discern the difference between the prayer which is only supplication, and that which takes its guerdon from the outstretched hand of Jesus. Too often our prayers seem like lost vessels; when, in point of fact, they have come to the quays richly freighted, but we have not been there to claim our own. Perhaps these rules may assist you to acquire this blessed art:

1. Be sure that what you ask is according to the mind of God, offered in some promise or precept of Holy Scripture.

2. Ask for it simply and reverently. Use the name of Jesus; that is, stand in Him, and plead for His glory.

3. Dare to believe that God does hear and answer your prayer altogether apart from the flow of emotion, or the rapture of conscious possession.

4. Go your way and reckon that God is faithful. Count on Him as bound to keep His truth.

F. B. MEYER

O God, Thou art my God;
early will I seek Thee.

P S A L M 6 3 : 1

Observe the eagerness implied in the time mentioned; he will not wait for noon or the cool eventide; he is up at cockcrowing to meet his God. Communion with God is so sweet that the chill of the morning is forgotten, and the luxury of the couch is despised. The morning is the time for dew and freshness, and the psalmist consecrates it to prayer and devout fellowship. The best of men have been betimes on their knees. The word "early" has not only the sense of early in the morning, but that of eagerness, immediateness. He who truly longs for God, longs for Him now.

C. H. S P U R G E O N

Early, my God, without delay,
I haste to seek Thy face;
My thirsty spirit faints away
Without Thy cheering grace.

Not all the blessings of a feast,
Can please my soul so well;
As when Thy richer grace I taste,
And in Thy presence dwell.

*Turn away mine eyes from
beholding vanity.*

PSALM 119:37

He had prayed about his heart, and one would have thought that the eyes would so surely have been influenced by the heart that there was no need to make them the objects of a special petition; but our author is resolved to make assurance doubly sure. If the eyes do not see, perhaps the heart may not desire; at any rate, one door of temptation is closed when we do not even look at the painted bauble. Sin first entered man's mind by the eye, and it is still a favorite gate for the incoming of Satan's allurements; hence the need of a double watch upon that portal. The prayer is not so much that the eyes may be shut as "turned away," for we need to have them open, but directed to right objects. . . . For fear he should forget himself and gaze with a lingering longing upon forbidden objects, he entreats the Lord to speedily turn away his eyes, hurrying him off from so dangerous a parley with iniquity.

C. H. SPURGEON

The prayer-life is hindered or helped by what the eyes behold, and by what the ears hear.

*But my God shall supply all your need
according to His riches in glory by Christ Jesus.*

*T*hough all believers in the Lord Jesus are not called upon to establish orphan houses, schools for poor children, etc., and trust in God for means, yet all believers according to the will of God concerning them in Christ Jesus, may cast, and ought to cast, all their care upon Him who careth for them, and need not be anxiously concerned about anything, as is plainly to be seen from 1 Peter 5:7; Philippians 4:6; Matthew 6:24, 25.

GEORGE MÜLLER

The life of prayer and faith is the secret of a life of abiding peace of heart. Many worry and are troubled because they have not learned to pray without ceasing, and in everything. At the same time many lives fail to be a rich blessing in the world because they are not lives of prayer for the world. We may well ask ourselves, Is my prayer-life really amounting to anything for the good of others?

But when he saw the wind boisterous, he was afraid;
and beginning to sink he cried, saying, Lord save me.
MATTHEW 14:30

*O*ffer ejaculatory petitions. Often send up brief, unspoken petitions. "A single cry for strength against sudden temptation or help in immediate work, a word of intercession for another, of thanksgiving, of joyful communion." You will thus acquire the habit of "praying always." Ephesians 6:18. Stonewall Jackson, asked about praying without ceasing, said, "I never raise a glass of water to my lips without asking God's blessing, nor seal a letter without putting a word of prayer under the seal, nor take a letter from the post without a brief sending of my thought heavenward, nor change my classes without a minute's petition on the cadets who come." "Don't you sometimes forget to do this?" "I scarcely can say that I do. The habit has become as fixed as breathing."

ABBIE C. MORROW

Even work in the service of God and of love is exhausting: we cannot bless others without power going from us; this must be renewed from above.

ANDREW MURRAY

Rejoice the soul of Thy servant: for unto Thee,
O Lord, do I lift up my soul.

P S A L M   8 6 : 4

*W*e may venture to ask and expect gladness if we are God's servants. All His creatures have a claim on Him for blessedness according to their capacity, so long as they stand where He has set them—and we, who have departed from that obedience which is joy, may yet, in penitent abasement, return to Him and ask that He would rejoice the soul of His servant. David's deepest repentance dared to ask, "make me to hear joy and gladness, that the bones which thou hast broken may rejoice." Our most troubled utterances of sore need, our signs and groans, should be accompanied with faith which feels the summer's sun of joy even in the midwinter of our pain and sees vineyards in the desert. We should believe in, hope and ask for more than bare deliverance—hard though it be to think that gladness is any more possible.

F. B. MEYER

Joyousness should characterize our prayer-life under all circumstances. Joy should ever be an accompaniment and an effect of prayer.

*And my servant Job shall pray for you: for him
will I accept. . . . And the Lord turned the captivity
of Job, when he prayed for his friends.*

J O B   4 2 : 8 ,   1 0

*A*nother and a most important phase of
prayer is intercession. What a work God
has set open for those who are His priests—intercessors! We find a wonderful expression in the prophecy
of Isaiah; God says, "Let him take hold of Me;" and
again, "There is none that stirreth up himself to take
hold of thee." In other passages God refers to the intercessors for Israel. Have you ever taken hold of God?
The church and the world need nothing so much as a
mighty Spirit of intercession to bring down the power
of God on earth. Pray for the descent from heaven of
the Spirit of intercession for a great prayer revival.

A N D R E W   M U R R A Y

Have you committed yourself to the ministry of intercession for your friends, and for the world? Learn from
Job's experience that when we pray for others God will
turn our captivity and prosper our souls. Selfishness
may be a bane in our prayer-life as elsewhere.

Hide not Thy face far from me; put not Thy servant away in anger: Thou has been my help; leave me not, neither forsake me, O God of my salvation.

P S A L M   2 7 : 9

*W*e are opposing God's method of working if our life has a tendency to incapacitate us for the enjoyment of prayer at all times. If by needless excess of worldly cares; if by inordinate desires, which render it impossible for us to accomplish our objects in life without such excess of care; if by frivolous habits; if by the reading of infidel or effeminate litera-ture; if by an indolent life; if by any self-indulgence in physical regimen—we render the habit of fragmentary prayer impracticable or unnatural to us, we are cross-ing the methods of God's working.

A U S T I N   P H E L P S

God's face is hid from us not because of something He puts before it, as by something in our own life which comes in between us and Him. The soul should be as directly in touch with God at all times as every tele-phone is with the central office, so that at any time communication may be made.

*Watch and pray, that ye enter
not into temptation.*

M A T T H E W   2 6 : 4 1

*T*he strongest and bravest men in build and muscle are often the weakest in resisting the appeals to momentary passion. Esau is mastered by the fragrance of a mess of pottage; Samson by the charms of a Philistine girl; Peter by the question of a servant. There is no strength apart from the strong Son of God.

And the appeals to sense come oftenest when we are least expecting them. When we say Peace and Safety, then sudden destruction comes. The foe creeps through the postern gate. The arrow penetrates the joints of the harness. The moment of crisis is the moment when we come in from the dangers of the chase to the home which promised us immunity from the attack. "Watch ye therefore, and pray always," that ye may be accounted worthy to escape all these things.

F. B. MEYER

By the weapon of all prayer we shall be protected from the fiery darts of the wicked one. Be careful never to go into life's conflict without it.

And thou, Solomon my son, know thou the God of thy father, and serve Him with a perfect heart and with a willing mind: for the Lord searcheth all hearts, and understandeth all the imaginations of the thoughts.

1   C H R O N I C L E S   2 8 : 9

*N*othing makes prayer so unreal as lack of honesty. If thought is sluggish and feeling cold, do not use the language of warm devotion. Say exactly what you mean, not more than you honestly purpose. But tell God the great truths you believe, the principles and purposes you really have, even if, for the moment, you do not feel them. This will bring a reality of things spiritual that will drive away seeming indifference.

H E N R Y   C H U R C H I L L   K I N G

The slightest selfishness, the least wrong motive, is seen by Him with whom we have to do. We need to be honest in our own self-examination in order to be honest before God in our praying. Oh to aim purely at God's glory in all our requests, and in all our living. A very small speck of dust may stop a watch, and a very trifling thing may hinder our prayers.

And it came to pass in those days, that He went out into a mountain to pray, and continued all night in prayer to God. And when it was day, He called unto Him His disciples: and of them He chose twelve, whom also He named apostles.

LUKE 6:12, 13

*W*e are prone to think that converse with Christian brethren, and the general round of Christian activity, especially when we are much busied with preaching the Word and visits to inquiring or needy souls, make up for the loss of aloneness with God in the secret place. We hurry to a public service with but a few minutes of private prayer, allowing precious time to be absorbed in social pleasures, restrained from withdrawing from others by a false delicacy, when to excuse ourselves for needful communion with God and His Word would have been perhaps the best witness possible to those whose company was holding us unduly! How often we rush from one public engagement to another without any proper interval for renewing our strength in waiting on the Lord, as though God cared more about the quantity than the quality of our service.

A. T. PIERSON

He that cometh to God must believe
that He is, and that He is a rewarder of them
that diligently seek Him.

H E B R E W S   1 1 : 6

*W*hile the prayer of faith is sure to succeed, our prayers, alas! too often resemble the mischievous tricks of children in a town, who knock at their neighbors' houses, and then run away. We often knock at mercy's door, and then run away, instead of waiting for an entrance and an answer. Thus we act as if we were afraid of having our prayers answered.

A   W E L S H   P R E A C H E R

It is the prayer into which the whole soul goes in an intensity of desire, that lays hold upon God. These indifferent, heartless, bloodless prayers that we offer and soon forget what we ask for count little with Him.

R .   A .   T O R R E Y

To play at praying as children play at ringing bells or knocking at doors is deserving of the severest condemnation, and yet how much of our praying is little less. We do not make a real business with God of it, and believe that He is a rewarder of them that diligently seek Him.

*I pray thee, let me go over, and see the good land that is
beyond Jordan, that goodly mountain, and Lebanon.
But the Lord was wroth with me for your sakes,
and would not hear me: and the Lord said unto me,
Let it suffice thee; speak no more unto me of this matter.*

D E U T E R O N O M Y 3 : 2 5 , 2 6

There are experiences with us all in which God
forgives our sin, but takes vengeance on our
inventions. We reap as we have sown. We suffer where
we have sinned. At such times our prayer is not literally answered. By the voice of the Spirit, by a spiritual
instinct, we become conscious that it is useless to pray
further. Though we pray, not thrice, but three hundred
times, the thorn is not taken away. But there is a sense
in which the prayer is answered. Our suffering is a lesson warning men in all after-time. We are permitted
from Pisgah's height to scan the fair land we long for,
and are then removed to a better. We have the answer
given to us in the after-time, as Moses, who had his
prayer gloriously fulfilled when he stood with Christ
on the Transfiguration Mount.

F. B. MEYER

Give us this day our daily bread.

M A T T H E W   6 : 1 1

Remove far from me vanity and lies;
give me neither poverty nor riches; feed me
with the food that is needful for me.

P R O V E R B S   3 0 : 8 ,   R . V .

here is always danger of going to extremes. Some people are so spiritual that they would take God out of the secular realm and leave it wholly to the Devil and the world. Now, just because Satan claims to be the god of this world God wants us to recognize Him in it and inscribe "Holiness to the Lord" upon everything we touch. Secular things are the only things that the world can understand, and when they see God meeting us in them our testimony speaks to the world with a force which they cannot feel in connection with our higher experience and more spiritual testimonies. . . . Let us therefore not hesitate to take Him for our bodies, for our business, for our finances, for our joys and sorrows and glorify the whole realm of nature and providence with the Lord of heaven.

A L L I A N C E   P A P E R

And it came to pass, when the vessels were full,
that she said unto her son, Bring me yet a vessel. And
he said unto her, There is not a vessel more.
And the oil stayed.

2   K I N G S   4 : 6

C hristians are in danger, when a revival has continued for some time, of praying less for its continuance, and of being less thankful for it. They seem to take it for granted that it will go on as a matter of course; their prayers grow less frequent and fervent, and their gratitude less lively, until at length a case of conversion, which would at first have electrified the whole church, produces scarcely any sensation at all. Now, when this is the case, a revival will certainly cease; for God never continues to bestow spiritual favors where they are not felt to be such.

EDWARD PAYSON

What is true of the church is equally true of the individual. When we cease to desire we cease to get. When we cease to make provision for larger things in our prayer-life, in our inner growth, in our work for Christ we shall receive no fuller blessing.

And Abraham drew near and said, Wilt
Thou also destroy the righteous with the wicked? . . .
Shall not the Judge of all the earth do right?

GENESIS 18:23, 25

*G*od granted Abraham's prayer so far as he
ventured to extend it. We know not what
would have been the answer, had he gone further. But
we have here the highest encouragement for intercessory prayer—to plead with God for wicked men, for
communities and nations that are far gone in sin.
Abraham received no denial. So far as we can see, it
was he who left off, and not God; yet we are to rest
humbly and trustfully upon God's good pleasure,
after all our prayer.

GEORGE BUSH

We shall seldom err in praying for too much; we far
too frequently err in praying for too little. We come far
short of the promises and of the willingness and power
of God. There is always a large balance to our credit
in the bank of heaven waiting for the exercise of our
faith in drawing it. "Expect great things from God."

Him that cometh to Me
I will in no wise cast out.
J O H N   6 : 3 7

*T*his man receiveth sinners," but He repulses
none. We come to Him in weakness and sin,
with trembling faith, and small knowledge, and slen-
der hope; but He does not cast us out. We come by
prayer, by prayer broken; with confession, and that
confession faulty, with praise, and that praise far short
of its merits; but He receives us. We come diseased,
polluted, worn out, and worthless; but He doth in no
wise cast us out. Let us come again today to Him who
never casts us out.

C. H. Spurgeon

This promise is very wide, "Him that cometh."
Anyone, no matter who they are, who really comes to
Christ will find acceptance and blessing. The main
thing is to get to Christ, to come indeed to Him. He
has pledged Himself not to cast out those who come.
Plead the promise. The fact that we have sinned should
not keep us away; indeed in that fact there is all the
more reason that we should come. Come today as
thou art and Christ will not turn you away.

*But the hour cometh, and now is, when the
true worshippers shall worship the Father in spirit
and in truth: for the Father seeketh
such to worship Him.*

J O H N   4 : 2 3

*G*od is seeking worshippers. The one thing above all else that He desires of men is worship. God desires obedience from men; He desires service; He desires prayer; He desires thanksgiving; He desires praise. But His supreme desire from men is worship. It is said, "We are saved that we may serve." It is true, but it is still more profoundly true that we are saved that we may worship. The whole work of redemption finds its culmination and completion in a body of men and women being found fit to worship God. Cf. Revelation 7:9-15, and Philippians 3:3, R.V.

R. A. TORREY

We may pray much without worshipping God, but prayer will find its freest access to the throne of grace, and will be accompanied by the fullest assurance and joy when it is preceded by a time of true worship of God. We need to spend more time in pure and simple worship, in bowing before God in silent and adoring contemplation of Himself.

For He is thy Lord; and worship thou Him.

P S A L M   4 5 : 1 1

*T*he worship of God is the soul bowing down before God in absorbed contemplation of Himself. Over and over do we read the words, "they bowed their heads and worshipped;" or "they fell down and worshipped." It has been well said that, "In prayer we are occupied with our needs; in thanksgiving we are occupied with our blessings; in worship we are occupied with Himself." God would not have us less occupied with our needs or present them less to Him. Neither would He have us less occupied with our blessings or return thanks less to Him for them; but He would have us, I am sure, more occupied with Himself in intelligent worship.

R. A. TORREY

As bearing on our prayer-life, the testimony of the man whom Jesus gave his sight to the importance of worship is very significant. "If any man be a worshipper of God him He heareth." John 9:31. Worship is the atmosphere in which prayer thrives best, and grows most heavenly and divine.

And being in an agony He prayed the more
earnestly: and His sweat was as it were great drops
of blood falling down to the ground.

L U K E   2 2 : 4 4

Only once is this word translated "agony" in the Bible and it is here. What depths open before us as we read this passage, and see what laboring in prayer means. It means seeing the world's sin somewhat as Christ saw it. It means seeing the world's need somewhat as Christ saw it. It means assenting utterly as Christ did, to God's judgment upon sin. And it means entering so into the will of God about the world's deliverance from sin, that for that end we are willing to lay down our lives. To true laboring in prayer there is necessary something of the Saviour's conception of sin, and an inner intimate fellowship with His sufferings. It is only after we have been in the garden with Him that we learn the deeper lessons of the school of prayer.

G E O R G E   C .   H .   M A C G R E G O R

How little, oh how little we know in experience what it is to be in agony in prayer. What deep, deep lessons in prayer we need yet to learn. Lord, teach us to pray.

I will give myself unto prayer.
P S A L M   1 0 9 : 4

She departed not from the temple, but served God
with fasting and prayers night and day.
L U K E   2 : 3 7

If we with earnest effort could succeed
To make our life one long connected prayer,
As lives of some have been and are;
If, never leaving Thee, we had no need
Our wandering spirits back again to lead.
Into Thy presence, but continue there,
Like angels standing on the highest stair
Of the sapphire throne—this were to pray, indeed.
But if distraction manifold prevail,
And if in this we must confess we fail,
Grant us to keep at least a prompt desire,
Continual readiness for prayer praise,
An altar heaped and waiting to take fire
With the least spark, and leap into a blaze.

T R E N C H

*R*eadiness for prayer" there may be, for as we
"walk in the Spirit" it will be easy at any time
to talk with our Lord, and have sweet fellowship with
Him. There should always be as great readiness for praise
as for prayer. David said: "I will bless the Lord at all times."

I also will keep thee from the
hour of temptation.

REVELATION 3:10

He is able to keep that which I have
committed unto Him.

2 TIMOTHY 1:12

*N*ot those men who have most principal or
most knowledge are the most secure, but
those who possess in their hearts the most of the Spirit
of devotion. No amount of resolving will help a man,
apart from the mood of mind that walks lovingly and
truly with God in constant prayerfulness. We must
guard the central magazine where is stored the pow-
der a spark may explode. Luther says, "The Devil
plagues and torments us in the place where we are the
most tender and weak. In Paradise he fell not upon
Adam but upon Eve."

D. W. FAUNCE

The Devil will be very ready to make his attacks when
we are off our guard, and we are never more off our
guard than when we neglect to pray. If it is true that "the
Devil trembles when he sees the weakest saint upon his
knees," it is undoubtedly equally true that he rejoices
when he sees a saint neglecting to get on his knees.

*And all Judah rejoiced at the oath: for they had
sworn with all their heart, and sought Him with
their whole desire; and He was found of them:
and the Lord gave them rest round about.*

2   C H R O N I C L E S   1 5 : 1 5

*T*here are some who often carry strong desires
in their heart, without bringing them to God
in the clear expression of definite and repeated prayer.
There are others who go to the Word and its promises
to strengthen their faith, but do not give sufficient
place to pointed asking of God which helps the soul
to the assurance that the matter has been put into
God's hands. Still others come in prayer with so many
requests and desires that it is difficult for themselves
to say what they really expect God to do.

A N D R E W   M U R R A Y

Our desires in prayer must be heart desires, definite
desires, expressed desires, desires in harmony with the
will of God. "Delight thyself also in the Lord, and He
shall give thee the desires of thine heart." Psalm 37:4.
"Prayer is the soul's sincere desire uttered or unex-
pressed."

*Let the words of my mouth, and the
meditation of my heart, be acceptable in Thy sight,
O Lord, my strength and my redeemer.*

P S A L M   1 9 : 1 4

*P*rayer is not a smooth expression, or a well contrived form of words; not the product of a ready memory, or rich invention, exerting itself in the performance. . . . The motion of the heart Godward, holy and divine affection, makes prayer real and lively, and acceptable to the living God, to whom it is presented; the pouring out of thy heart to Him that made it, and therefore hears it, and understands what it speaks, and how it is moved and affected in calling on Him. It is not the gilded paper, and the good writing of a petition that prevails with a king, but the moving sense of it; and to the king that discerns the heart, heart-sense is the sense of all, and that which He alone regards; He listens to hear what that speaks, and takes all as nothing where that is silent. All other excellence on prayer is but the outside and fashion of it; that is the life of it.

R .   L E I G H T O N

Learn to pray in the Spirit; let thy prayers be the outgoing of thy inner spiritual being.

And Jacob said, O God of my father Abraham,
and God of my father Isaac, the Lord which saidst
unto me, Return unto thy country, and to
thy kindred and I will deal well with
thee. Deliver me I pray Thee.

GENESIS 32 : 9 – 11

*T*here are many healthy symptoms in that prayer. In some respects it may serve as a mold into which our own spirits may pour themselves, when melted in the fiery furnace of sorrow.

He began by quoting God's promise: "Thou saidst." He did so twice (9 and 12). Ah, he had got God in his power then! God puts Himself within our reach in His promises; and when we can say to Him, "Thou saidst" He cannot say nay. He must do as He has said. If Herod was so particular for his oath's sake, what will not our God be? Be sure in prayer, to get your feet well on a promise; it will give you purchase enough to force open the gates of heaven, and to take it by force.

F. B. MEYER

Climb to the treasure-house of blessing on a ladder made of divine promises. By a promise as by a key open the door to the riches of God's grace and favor.

In all thy ways acknowledge Him,
and He shall direct thy paths.

P R O V E R B S 3 : 6

Never trust your own judgment. When your common sense is most sure of the rightness of a certain course of action, it will be best to make assurance doubly sure by lifting up your soul to God, that it may dim with His No, or glisten with His Yes. When voices within or without would hasten you to decide on the strength of your own conclusion, then be careful to refer the whole matter from the lower court of your own judgment to the Supreme tribunal of God's. If there is any doubt or hesitation left after such a reference, be sure that as yet the time has not come for you to understand all God's will. Under such circumstances—wait. Throw the responsibility of the pause and all it may involve on God; and dare still to wait. . . . If you trust God absolutely, it is for Him to give you clear directions as to what you should do. And when the time for action arrives, He will have given you such unmistakable indications of His will that you will not be able to mistake them or err therein.

F. B. MEYER

*And, behold, there was a man in Jerusalem,
whose name was Simeon, and the same man was just
and devout, waiting for the consolation of Israel:
and the Holy Ghost was upon him.*

LUKE 2:25

*W*hile Simeon prayed fervently, he waited patiently; he mocked not God by asking for that for which he did not wait. Many would be rich in spiritual things, if they could grasp them all at once; and would soon empty heaven's exchequer of all its wealth, if prayer and patience were not required in exchange. Many will wait in the vestibule of royalty for the favors of the great; but how few, even of professing Christians, will wait for the notice of the King of kings and Lord of lords. The merchant waits for his grains, and the farmer for his crops; the physician for his patient, and the lawyer for his fee; the poet for his inspiration, and the artist for his fame; while the pearl of heaven is thought by many to be too poor a prize to bring them to their knees for a single hour, or to keep them at the gates of wisdom for a single day.

W. P. BALFERN

And when David inquired of the Lord,
He said, thou shalt not go up, but fetch a
compass behind them, and come upon them
over against the mulberry trees.

2 S A M U E L   5 : 2 3

*A*gain the Philistines came up to assert their olden supremacy, and again David waited on the Lord for direction. It was well that he did so, because the plan of campaign was not as before. Those that rely on God's cooperation must be careful to be in constant touch with Him. The aid which was given yesterday in one form will be given tomorrow in another. In the first battle the position of the Philistines was carried by assault; in the second it was turned by ambush. To have reversed the order, or to have acted on the two occasions identically, would have missed the method and movement of those divine legions who acted as David's invincible allies.

F . B . M E Y E R

Yesterday we prayed and gained the victory in a certain way; today we need to pray again, for God's method for yesterday may not be His method for today.

With my whole heart have I sought Thee.

PSALM 119:10

His heart had gone after God Himself: he had not only desired to obey His laws, but to commune with His person. This is a right royal search and pursuit, and well may it be followed with the whole heart. The surest mode of cleansing the way of our life is to seek after God Himself, and to endeavor to abide in fellowship with Him. It is pleasant to see how the writer's heart turns distinctly and directly to God. He had been considering an important truth in the preceding verse, but here he so powerfully feels the presence of his God that he speaks to Him, and prays to Him as one who is near.

C. H. SPURGEON

True prayer gives the Giver Himself a larger place in its thoughts and desires than the gifts He bestows. Having Him the soul has all things. Finding her bridegroom the bride gains his riches as well. "He that spared not His own Son, but delivered Him up for us all, how shall He not with Him freely give us all things." Romans 8:32. Christ Himself should ever be the supreme desire in our prayers.

Remove from me reproach and contempt.

P S A L M   1 1 9 : 2 2

*T*he best way to deal with a slander is to pray about it; God will either remove it, or remove the sting from it. Our own attempts at clearing ourselves are usually failures; we are like the boy who wished to remove the blot from his copy, and by his bungling made it ten times worse. When we suffer from a libel it is better to pray about it than to go to law over it, or even to demand an apology from the inventor. O ye who are reproached, take your matters before the highest court, and leave them with the judge of all the earth.

C. H. SPURGEON

A vindictive spirit, a determination to "get even" with those who injure us, is destructive to the spirit of prayer. How watchful we need to be at this point, how necessary that we learn to put our case in God's hands. It will greatly help us to overcome a desire to avenge ourselves when others reproach us if we will begin to pray for them. Remember it is written, "Vengeance is mine; I will repay, saith the Lord."

And it came to pass, that, as He was praying
in a certain place, when He ceased, one of His disci-
ples said unto Him, Lord teach us to pray,
as John also taught his disciples.

LUKE 11:1

*F*ive grand conditions of prevailing prayer. 1. Entire dependence upon the merits and meditation of the Lord Jesus Christ, as the only ground of any claim for blessing. See John 14:13, 14, 15:16, etc.

2. Separation from all known sin. If we regard iniquity in our hearts, the Lord will not hear us, for it would be sanctioning sin. Psalm 66:18.

3. Faith in God's word of promise as confirmed by His oath. Not to believe Him is to make Him both a liar and a perjurer. Hebrews 11:6; 6:13–20.

4. Asking in accordance with His will. Our motives must be godly; we must not seek any gift of God to consume it upon our lusts. 1 John 5:13; James 4:3.

5. Importunity in supplication. There must be waiting on God, and waiting for God. Luke 18:1–10.

A. T. PIERSON

*Roll thy way upon the Lord. Trust also in Him
and He shall bring it to pass.*

PSALM 37:5 R.V. MARGIN

*A man's goings are established of the Lord,
and he delighteth in his way.*

PSALM 37:23 R.V.

A quiet hour spent alone with God at the beginning of the day is the best beginning for the toils and cares of active business. A brief season of prayer, looking above for wisdom and grace and strength, and seeking for an outpouring of the Holy Spirit, helps us to carry our religion into the business of the day. It brings joy and peace within the heart. And as we place all our concerns in the care and keeping of the Lord, faithfully striving to do His will, we have a joyful trust that however dark or discouraging events may appear, our Father's hand is guiding everything, and will give the wisest direction to all our toils.

AUTHOR UNKNOWN

Our Heavenly Father may not show us very much of the way along which He is leading us; let us be content and trustful as He leads us step by step. Pray for light for the next step, and leave the future in His hands.

And Jacob was left alone; and there wrestled a man with him until the breaking of the day.

GENESIS 32:24

There are times when, if you would prevail with God, you must go alone. Abraham left Sarah when he pleaded for Sodom. (Genesis 18:22, 23.) Moses was by himself at the wilderness bush. (Exodus 3:1–5.) Joshua was alone when the Lord came to him. (Joshua 1:1.) Gideon and Jephthah were by themselves when commissioned to save Israel. (Judges 6:11, 11:29.) Elijah and Elisha raised a child from the dead, alone. (1 Kings 17:19; 2 Kings 4:33.) Cornelius was praying by himself when the angel came to him. (Acts 10:2.) No one was with Peter on the housetop when he was instructed to go to the Gentiles. (Acts 10:9.) John the Baptist was alone in the wilderness (Luke 1:80), and John the beloved, alone in Patmos, when nearest God. (Revelation 1:9.)

ABBIE C. MORROW

Many times in these daily thoughts is our attention called to the importance of being alone with God in prayer. It cannot be overemphasized.

*I pray not that Thou shouldest take
them out of the world, but that Thou
shouldst keep them from the evil.*

J O H N   1 7 : 1 5

*Neither pray I for these alone, but for them also
which shall believe on Me through their word.*

J O H N   1 7 : 2 0

*D*o we pray for the perfect unity of the church of Christ, for its deliverance from Laodicean lukewarmness, yea, for its complete redemption and glorification? Do we pray that Christendom may be freed from the apostasy and heresies of the last days, from the multifarious forms of occultism, demon-possession, and demon-worship? Do we pray that the awful tales of crime, drunkenness, vice and every form of sin may be stemmed, that the millions of lost souls groping in the darkness of heathenism may have the light of life, that the groaning creation may be emancipated from the thralldom of sin and the Devil, and that righteousness may cover the earth even as the waters cover the mighty deep? Do we pray "Thy Kingdom Come," that the kingdoms of this world may become the Kingdom of our Lord, and of His Christ?

J. A. F R A S E R

*And be ready in the morning, and come up
in the morning unto Mount Sinai, and present thyself there to Me in the top of the Mount. And
no man shall come up with thee.*

E X O D U S 3 4 : 2 , 3

We must dare to be alone. . . . "When thou prayest enter into thy closet, and when thou hast shut thy door, pray to thy Father which is in secret." Jacob must be left alone if the Angel of God is to whisper in his ear the mystic name of Shiloh; Daniel must be alone if he is to see the celestial vision; John must be banished to Patmos if he is deeply to take and firm to keep "the print of heaven." The isolated cloud alone contains in its bosom the mighty thunderstorm; that which is stranded on the mountain slope is soon robbed of its electricity. . . . Let the first moments of the day, when the heart is fresh, be given to God. Never see the face of man till you have seen the King. Dare to be much alone on the Mount.

F. B. MEYER

It has been well said, "Christlike praying in secret will be the secret of Christlike living in public."

*If any man see his brother sinning a sin,
not unto death, he shall ask, and God will give him
life for them that sin not unto death.*

1 JOHN 5:16 R.V.

*B*eloved friend, you do not know what you could do if you would give yourself up to intercession. It is a work that a sick one lying on a bed year by year may do in power. It is a work that a poor one who has hardly a penny to give to a missionary society can do day by day. It is a work that a young girl who is in her father's house and has to help in the housekeeping can do by the Holy Spirit.

God wants us, Christ wants us, because He has to do a work; the work of Calvary is to be done in our hearts; we are to sacrifice our lives to pleading with God for men. Oh, let us yield ourselves day by day and ask God that it may please Him to let His Holy Spirit work in us.

ANDREW MURRAY

The boundless possibilities of a life of intercession, the unspeakable need, should powerfully move us to give ourselves to prayer.

*And the apostles gathered themselves together
unto Jesus, and told Him all things, both what
they had done, and what they had taught.*

M A R K   6 : 3 0

*T*he disciples, we read, "returned to Jesus and told Him all things, both what they had done and what they had taught." I think that if we would, every evening, come to our Master's feet and tell Him where we have been, what we have done, what we have said and what were the motives by which we have been actuated, it would have a salutary effect upon our whole conduct. While reading over each day's page of life with the consciousness that He was reading it with us, we should detect many errors and defects which would otherwise pass unnoticed.

E D W A R D   P A Y S O N

Tell Jesus. Tell Him of thy joys as well as of thy sorrows; tell Him of thy successes as well as of thy failures. Tell Him of thy companions, friendships, helpful books, what you have said, thought, seen, done. Tell it all to Jesus. And when you tell Him do not forget to thank Him for every moment of joy, every comfort, all the help you have received through these channels.

Herein is My Father glorified, that ye bear
much fruit; so shall ye be My disciples.

J O H N 1 5 : 8

*N*ow we know the great reason why we have
not had power in faith to pray prevailingly.
Our life was not as it should have been; simple down-
right obedience, abiding fruitfulness was not its chief
mark. And with our whole heart we approve of the
divine appointment: men to whom God is to give such
influence in the rule of the world; as at their request to
do what otherwise would not have taken place, men
whose will is to guide the path in which God's will is
to work must be men who have themselves learned
obedience, whose loyalty and submission to authority
must be above all suspicion. Our whole soul approves
the law: obedience and fruit-bearing, the path to prevailing prayer.

A N D R E W M U R R A Y

The Lord Jesus is our example in living the prayer-life.
He glorified the Father on the earth. In all His living
and in all His praying this was His aim, hence the
power of His life. As we live and pray purely that God
may be glorified we shall prevail.

If ye abide in Me, and My words abide in you, ye shall ask what ye will, and it shall be done unto you.

JOHN 15:7

What is it to abide in Christ? It is to continue in living union with Him. To bear the same relation to Him that the living healthy branch, the continuously fruit-bearing branch, does to the vine. This branch has no independent life of its own. Its sap and vigor all come from the vine. Its leaves, buds, blossoms, fruit are all the product of the life of the vine in it. So we abide in Christ insofar as we have no independent life of our own. Insofar as we do not seek to have any thoughts, plans, feelings, purposes, works, fruits of our own, but let Christ think His thoughts, feel His feelings, purpose His purposes, work His works, bear His fruit in us. When we do this, and insofar as we do this, we may ask whatsoever we will and it shall be done.

R. A. TORREY

Is it not worth all that it involves to abide in Christ to have the blessed privilege of living a prayer-life in which we shall receive day by day that for which we ask?

*Continue in prayer, and watch in the
same with thanksgiving.*

C O L O S S I A N S　4 : 2

*S*teadfast continuance in prayer must never be
hindered by the want of sensible enjoyment;
in fact, it is a safe maxim that the less joy, the more
need. Cessation of communion with God, for whatever cause, only makes the more difficult its resump-
tion and the recovery of the prayer habit and prayer
spirit; whereas the persistent outpouring of supplication, together with continued activity in the service of
God, soon brings back the lost joy. Whenever, therefore, one yields to spiritual depression so as to aban-
don, or even to suspend closet communion or
Christian work, the Devil triumphs.

A. T. PIERSON,
IN *GEORGE MÜLLER OF BRISTOL*

Never do we need so much to pray as when we have
the least inclination to. When we do not feel like praying we should pray till we do. It is a good help to
awaken the spirit of prayer to read some book on
answers to prayer. As we consider the wonders God
has wrought in answer to prayer we too shall be moved
to pray.

And he was sore athirst, and called on the Lord, and said, Thou hast given this great deliverance into the hand of Thy servant: and now shall I die for thirst, and fall into the hand of the uncircumcised?

JUDGES   15 : 18

*S*amson has been divinely helped by the power of the Spirit of God in slaying a thousand Philistines; would not God now quench his thirst? Having done the greater work for him, would God not do the less? This is good reasoning in prayer, and it is a sort of reasoning that God's children may use. If God has done the great thing for thee in answer to prayer will He not do the less? Having saved thy soul and delivered thee from the power of sin, and of the enemy, will He not supply thy temporal needs, and care for thy body? Having brought us out of darkness into light will He not now keep us as children of light? If when we were faraway He brought us nigh and gave unto us the Spirit of adoption, will He not now bless us with all spiritual blessings in heavenly things in Christ? What God has already done should encourage us to pray in faith for what we need now.

CHARLES A. COOK

*Now the God of hope fill you with all joy
and peace in believing, that ye may abound in hope,
through the power of the Holy Ghost.*
R O M A N S   1 5 : 1 3

*T*his way of living has often been the means of reviving the work of grace in my heart, when I have been getting cold; and it also has been the means of bringing me back again to the Lord, after I have been backsliding. For it will not do—it is not possible to live in sin, and at the same time, by communion with God, to draw down from heaven everything one needs for the life that now is. . . . Answer to prayer, obtained in this way, has been the means of quickening my soul, and filling me with much joy.

G E O R G E   M Ü L L E R

It is well to have some special responsibility resting upon us in the Lord's work, as George Muller did, which will necessitate our praying. Thus will we be kept in touch with the source of all spiritual blessing, and our spiritual strength and joy will be renewed. We do not feel the need of prayer more than we do, because we have not undertaken any great thing for God. We are thus missing a double blessing.

*But Moses' hands were heavy; and they took a stone,
and put it under him, and he sat thereon; and Aaron
and Hur stayed up his hands, the one on the one side,
and the other on the other side; and his hands were
steady until the going down of the sun.*

E X O D U S   1 7 : 1 2

According to the prayers of a church are the successes of the church. Are they maintained, the banner floats on to victory; are they languid and depressed, the foe achieves a transient success. Let us then learn to pray filling our Rephidims with strong crying and tears, obtaining by faith for ourselves and others victories which no prowess of our own could win. These shall encourage us like nothing beside, filling our heart with joy, our lips with songs, and our hands with the spoil of the foe. What deliverances might we win for our dear ones, and all others who are strongly molested by the flesh, if only we were more often found on the top of the hill with the uplifted rod of prayer in our steadied hands!

F. B. MEYER

Learn to be an Aaron or a Hur.

Behold he prayeth.

ACTS 9:11

So I prayed to the God of heaven.

NEHEMIAH 2:4

The prayer-life of the Christian is the true gauge of all the rest of his life. As the water in the gauge-glass and in the boiler always remain at the same level, the water in the one never rising higher than the water in the other, so no man's outer life of activity ever rises above his inner life of prayer. As a man prays so is he. No man ever becomes a better Christian than he is in his prayer-life. No matter how zealous, how busy, how benevolent, how good a name he may have among men as a Christian worker, teacher, preacher, he is no better than he is when he is alone with God in prayer. What he is and does there in secret will appear openly. If he is weak, lacking, powerless there, he will be weak and lacking in spiritual power at every other point in his Christian character and activities. Everything as to what a Christian becomes, and as to what he accomplishes for God and His Kingdom depends upon prayer as it depends on nothing else in all the world.

CHARLES A. COOK

Acquaint now thyself with Him, and be at peace:
thereby good shall come unto thee.

J O B 2 2 : 2 1

*M*en not only need the quiet hour to get acquainted with one's self, and with one's task in life, but to get acquainted with God. A young lady said to me, "After all is it not just as well to talk about God as to talk to God?" I replied, "How is it about your mother? Is it just as well to talk about your mother as it is to talk to her?" "Oh, no," she said, "that is different. Mother talks back, you know." Precisely; that is part of Christian prayer—giving God a chance to talk with you, and not simply insisting on talking to Him. Prayer is not spreading our wants before Him, and running away in a hurry before He has time to say anything to us. Prayer is pouring out our needs before Him, and waiting until out of the infinite fullness, and peace, and power, there come back to us glimpses of duty, revelations of truth, equipment for service. Oh, stop doing for God sometimes, and let God do for you. Stop talking to God sometimes, and let Him talk to you.

W. H. P. FAUNCE

Give ear to my words, O Lord,
Consider my meditation.

P S A L M 5 : 1

For out of the abundance of my
meditation have I spoken hitherto.

1 S A M U E L 1 : 1 6

*D*o we not miss very much of the sweetness and efficacy of prayer by a want of careful meditation before it, and of hopeful expectation after it? We too often rush into the presence of God without forethought or humility. We are like men who present themselves before a king without a petition, and what wonder is it that we often miss the end of prayer? We should be careful to keep the stream of meditation always running: for this is the water to drive the mill of prayer. It is idle to pull up the flood-gates of a dry brook, and then hope to see the wheel revolve. . . . Prayer is the work of the Holy Spirit, but He works by means. . . . Let not our prayers and praises be the flashes of a hot and hasty brain, but the steady burning of a well-kindled fire.

C. H. SPURGEON

Meditation upon the Word of God, upon the promises to the prayerful, upon the answers to prayer recorded in the Bible, will keep the fires burning upon the altar of prayer.

Blessed be the Lord, because He hath heard the voice of my supplications. The Lord is my strength and my shield; my heart trusted in Him, and I am helped: therefore my heart greatly rejoiceth; and with my song will I praise Him.

PSALM 28:6, 7

Lord, what a change within us one short hour
Spent in Thy presence will prevail to make,
What heavy burdens from our bosoms take,
What parched grounds refresh, as with a shower!
We kneel and all around us seem to lower;
We rise, and all, the distant and the near,
Stands forth in sunny outline, brave and clear;
We kneel, how weak, we rise, how full of power.
Why, therefore, should we do ourselves this wrong,
Or others—that we are not always strong.
That we are ever overcome with care,
That we should ever weak or heartless be,
Anxious or troubled, when with us is prayer,
And joy, and strength, and courage are with Thee.

TRENCH

*P*rayer has a transforming power because it brings us into a pure atmosphere, and to a new point of view. It is not always that anything is changed; only through prayer we see things as we never saw them before. We are different in our attitude and so get the light and strength and blessing.

Thou art worthy, O Lord, to receive
glory and honour and power.

REVELATION 4 : 11

We do not sufficiently often forget our own petty wants and anxieties, and launch down our tiny rivulet, until we are borne out into the great ocean of praise, which is ever breaking in music around the person of Jesus. Praise is one of the greatest acts of which we are capable; and it is most like the service of heaven. There they ask for naught, for they have all and abound; but throughout the cycles of glory the denizens of those bright worlds fill them with praise. And why should not earthly tasks be wrought to the same music? Let a part of our private and public devotion be even dedicated to the praise of Jesus; when we shall break forth into some hymn, or psalm, or spiritual song, singing and praising Christ with angels and archangels and all the host of the redeemed.

F. B. MEYER

Praise ye the Lord. Praise Him for His mighty acts; praise Him according to His excellent greatness. Let everything that hath breath praise the Lord. Praise ye the Lord.